Sociology of
Crime & Deviance

Jill Swale

Philip Allan Updates, an imprint of Hodder Education, an Hachette UK company, Market Place, Deddington, Oxfordshire OX15 0SE

Orders

Bookpoint Ltd, 130 Milton Park, Abingdon, Oxfordshire, OX14 4SB
tel: 01235 827720
fax: 01235 400454
e-mail: uk.orders@bookpoint.co.uk
Lines are open 9.00 a.m.–5.00 p.m., Monday to Saturday, with a 24-hour message answering service. You can also order through the Philip Allan Updates website: www.philipallan.co.uk

© Philip Allan Updates 2007

ISBN 978-1-84489-633-2

Printed in Spain

Hachette UK's policy is to use papers that are natural, renewable and recyclable products and made from wood grown in sustainable forests. The logging and manufacturing processes are expected to conform to the environmental regulations of the country of origin.

P01952

Contents

Introduction

Sociologists have been trying to explain crime for about 150 years. This book considers the widely conflicting perspectives that sociologists have on crime, and also their suggested solutions. Examples from recent news are used. In the postmodern world, we can no longer focus exclusively on British crime and I hope you will find the exploration of global, state and green crime particularly interesting.

Chapter 1 opens with competing definitions of crime and deviance and examines consensus perspectives, which contrast starkly with the Marxist views in Chapter 2. Chapter 3 explores theories of social construction; synoptic links with media and health topics are made. Studies of youth subcultures and recent left-wing theories, frequently centred on juvenile crime, are the subjects of Chapter 4.

The immediate relevance of sociology is highlighted in Chapter 5, which begins with considerations of ethnicity and crime in the UK, and then widens out to consider global terrorism, state crime and crimes by transnational companies. Links between gender and crime are discussed in Chapter 6. Chapter 7 considers environmental and New Right theories; current strategies of situational crime prevention are highlighted. Chapter 8 draws together, and expands upon, the problems of researching crime and explores different approaches to the study of suicide.

While reading the chapters in chronological order is recommended, there is a glossary to enable you to look up explanations you may have by-passed.

My aim is to bring the sociology of crime and deviance to life. Early theories and influential studies are explored in enough detail to provide material for examination essays. The tasks invite you to apply the perspectives to news events and recent research. I have included more detail about how the studies were conducted than appears in most textbooks because this provides human interest and makes findings easier to evaluate, as well as providing information for methods-related questions. Suggestions for your own research, examination practice and highlighted synoptic links with other topics are included to help you use the material to full advantage.

I hope you find the study of crime and deviance as fascinating as I do.

Jill Swale

Crime, deviance and consensus

What is meant by crime?

What picture comes into your head when you think about crime? What sort of person is committing the crime? Who is the victim? What kind of crime is taking place?

If asked to sketch a crime, most people draw street crimes such as murder, assault and mugging. The imagined offender is usually male and often young and working class. The victims vary, but are often female or elderly. Try this out on friends to see if you obtain similar results.

This experiment highlights the way crime is socially constructed. We have a mental picture of typical crime because of the way it is discussed in the media and in society as a whole. Marxists would say that capitalist ideology leads us to blame the poor for property crimes and ignore huge financial swindles carried out by those controlling large corporations. We are unlikely to consider industrial pollution as a crime, yet it may blight more lives than street crime. Other sociologists ask why female criminality receives so little attention.

Crime is defined as behaviour that breaks the laws of a society. There are many other forms of crime apart from the street scenarios that first come to mind, so explanations of crime are also diverse. Various groups of sociologists argue that crime is necessary; they justify the acts of criminals or blame the police for making crime worse! This book encourages you to re-examine the nature of crime and to explore conflicting explanations.

What is meant by deviance?

Deviance is behaviour that differs from the norms of a particular group or society. It is considered abnormal and may be socially unacceptable, although some deviant acts are harmless, merely eccentric or exceptionally good. It is unusual never to be absent from school, so such behaviour deviates from the norm. However, sociologists are usually more interested in stigmatised or anti-social forms of behaviour that constitute social problems:

- By behaving abnormally, deviants may become victims of persecution.
- Deviance may be a response to society's failure to provide for those people's needs.
- Joining a deviant subculture may lead to deviance amplification. Members may become increasingly detached from the rest of society.

This implies that deviance is unde-sirable. However, Howard Becker (*Outsiders*, 1963) suggests that acts are not *intrinsically* deviant but are defined as such by powerful labellers. Influential people decide a certain act is not acceptable and others are persuaded to avoid it.

There is no logical reason why wearing socks with sandals should be a deviant act. Recently, however, young people decided that this was not the thing to do. Now everyone has to accept this arbitrary fashion ruling or risk ridicule!

Wilmar Photography/Alamy

Socks with sandals — a fashion faux pas or an act of deviance?

Task 1.1

Decide which of the following acts are crimes in present-day Britain, which are deviant, which are both criminal and deviant and which are neither:

- stuttering
- driving a few miles per hour above the speed limit
- small-scale tax evasion
- under-age drinking in public houses
- homosexuality between consenting adults
- committing suicide
- dyeing one's hair green
- being present when someone is taking illegal drugs
- spending money on holidays when others live in absolute poverty
- being naked in the bath
- being naked in the street
- joining a religious cult

Task 1.1 demonstrates the importance of context. Nakedness is not intrinsically deviant; it is acceptable privately because societal judgements are not involved. A nudist club could be viewed as a miniature society with different norms. Likewise, there are different rules for young children, who might play naked on British beaches. However, different cultures have different norms and ultra-Orthodox Jewish girls might stay completely covered, even on a beach.

Some offences, such as speeding and tax evasion, may be so common as not to be statistically deviant; taking ecstasy was allegedly the norm at acid-house parties. Suicide, homosexuality and mental illness are deviant because they are not majority experiences. Notice that the word 'deviant' is used neutrally in sociology and does not imply moral judgement.

Spending money on holidays when others live in absolute poverty is neither deviant nor illegal. However, Marxist sociologists regard this type of behaviour as one of the evils of capitalism. Angela Davis, a member of the Communist Party and the Black Panthers in the 1970s, argued that the real criminals are those who steal the world's wealth from ordinary working people. This view forms a *synoptic link to world sociology*.

Angela Davis suggested being prosperous in a poor world was theft

The issues of who defines an act as deviant and who decides what should be illegal have been much debated by social constructionists, Marxists, functionalists and feminists.

Consensus views of why people conform

Emile Durkheim made influential comments on crime and social control in developed societies in *The Rules of Sociological Method*, written in 1895. As a French functionalist, Durkheim was interested in why people conform to the demands of the society into which they are born. Though we view ourselves as individuals, we often have little choice but to abide by the prevailing norms.

I am not obliged to speak French with my fellow countrymen nor to use the legal currency, but I cannot possibly do otherwise. If I tried to escape this necessity, my attempt would fail miserably.

E. Durkheim, *The Rules of Sociological Method* (1895)

Laws and customs define appropriate behaviour and they have 'coercive power' over us. This constraint is felt only slightly when we conform. However, if we violate a law or custom, our behaviour will meet with a **negative sanction** (punishment or discouragement), either formal or informal, depending on the seriousness of the breach.

The public conscience exercises a check on every act which offends it by means of the surveillance it exercises over the conduct of citizens, and the appropriate penalties at its disposal. In many cases the constraint is less violent, but nevertheless it always exists. If I do not submit to the conventions of society, if in my dress I do not conform to the customs observed in my country and my class, the ridicule I provoke, the social isolation in which I am kept, produce, although in an attenuated form, the same effects as a punishment in the strict sense of the word.

E. Durkheim, *The Rules of Sociological Method* (1895)

Task 1.2 makes *synoptic links between social control and education.*

Task 1.2

Think of examples of sanctions that teachers use to shape students' behaviour, using the following sanction categories:

- formal, positive
- formal, negative
- informal, positive
- informal, negative

To help you, an example from a different context has been provided for each.

Sanctions	Positive	Negative
Formal	Bravery award	Parking fine
Informal	Being thanked	Being laughed at

Durkheim called society's constraints over individuals — such as early socialisation, education, legal and moral regulations, customs, economic systems and religious faiths — **social facts**.

> All education is a continuous effort to impose on the child ways of seeing, feeling and acting which he could not have arrived at spontaneously. From the very first hours of his life, we compel him to eat, drink and sleep at regular hours; we constrain him to cleanliness, calmness and obedience; later we exert pressure upon him in order that he may learn proper consideration for others, respect for customs and conventions, the need for work etc. If, in time, this constraint ceases to be felt, it is because it gradually gives rise to habits and to internal tendencies that render constraint unnecessary.
>
> E. Durkheim, *The Rules of Sociological Method* (1895)

Society's beliefs and practices are reinforced by each generation. They are passed down to the young by parents, teachers and other **agents of socialisation**. Values become internalised in every individual's mind as the 'collective conscience'. Moreover, actions that we regard as personal choices are often influenced by contemporary norms. This agreement about values is a **consensus** and creates an **integrated** society.

> Currents of opinion, with an intensity varying according to the time and place, impel certain groups either to more marriages, for example, or to more suicides, or to a higher or lower birth rate etc. These currents are plainly social facts.
>
> E. Durkheim, *The Rules of Sociological Method* (1895)

Though, hopefully, suicide is never likely to become a majority activity, there have been contexts in which it has become socially acceptable and, therefore, more common. For example, in the Second World War, Japanese kamikaze pilots crashed their planes into warships. Suicide bombings in the UK and elsewhere remind us that, among certain groups, even such horrific acts meet with collective approval.

Is crime inevitable? Durkheim's view

Durkheim observed that crime is present in all societies, because there will always be people who commit acts that offend others. In this sense, crime is 'normal', although the individuals who commit it are deviant. Durkheim made a more intriguing statement:

> To classify crime among the phenomena of normal sociology is not to say merely that it is an inevitable, although regrettable, phenomenon due to the incorrigible wickedness of men; it is to affirm that it is a factor in public health, an integral part of all healthy societies.
>
> E. Durkheim, *The Rules of Sociological Method* (1895)

All society's members cannot share the same sentiments about every possible type of potentially offensive behaviour because environmental and hereditary factors influence people differently. Moreover, societies need to progress. If conformity were too strong, all criticism would be repressed, resulting in stagnation. Innovation generates not only positive reforms by idealists but also the originality of criminals. Even then, crime is not necessarily regrettable.

> How many times, indeed, it is only an anticipation of future morality — a step towards what will be!
>
> E. Durkheim, *The Rules of Sociological Method* (1895)

Durkheim cited Socrates, condemned in Athens for his independence of thought, yet since applauded as a great philosopher. A recent example is Nelson Mandela, imprisoned for 27 years for opposing South Africa's apartheid system. When the regime changed, his stand against racism was recognised as heroic and he became the country's first black president.

Task 1.3

- Think of acts that were once regarded as crimes in Britain but which no longer are.
- Have there been other political protesters who, like Mandela, were later regarded as heroes or heroines?

Despite acknowledging that acts viewed as crimes may be regarded more favourably by later generations, Durkheim emphasised that he did not condone crime. Like pain in the body of society, it helps to preserve the organism, but is nevertheless unpleasant. Punishment is a social reaction to the offensiveness of crime and reinforces collective sentiments. Abhorrence would diminish if such acts went unpunished and more offences would follow. Nowadays, the media play an important role in drawing the public together in horror against acts such as racist murder and paedophilia.

Durkheim's view of anomie

Durkheim's belief that society's constraints over its members are usually beneficial was fundamentally conservative. People need to cooperate because they are mutually dependent, particularly in densely populated modern societies with complex divisions of labour. Yet the diversity, mobility and questioning of traditional values in such societies is likely to cause anomie, a state of moral confusion and normlessness, in which rates of crime and acts of deviance, such as suicide, may increase. Though a total absence of crime would suggest a repressive, stagnating society, a high crime rate indicates social breakdown and lack of integration. To maintain order for their own safety, individuals need to bow to the consensus, rather than follow their own whims.

In a footnote, Durkheim acknowledged that constraint by society is acceptable if its influence is 'intellectual or moral', but not if exercised by stronger or wealthier individuals and maintained by violence. To Marxists, this point needs more than a footnote. Their major argument is that people are oppressed by powerful capitalists and those who resist them are branded as criminals. This dramatically contrasting perspective will be explored shortly.

Merton and anomie

Robert K. Merton shared Durkheim's interest in conformity and deviance but developed his concept of anomie in a specific context. In *Social Theory and Social Structure* (1968), Merton distinguished his approach from Durkheim's. As a functionalist, Durkheim took a macro view of whole societies and generalised without always providing empirical evidence. Merton described his own theory as middle range. This meant that he was collecting data grounded in observable phenomena — the social mechanisms that influence people to behave in various ways — and connecting his findings with social structures more than a microsociologist would. The latter might, for example, observe only one gang.

Merton asked why the frequency and types of deviance varied between social groups.

> Our primary aim is to discover how some social structures exert a definite pressure upon certain persons in the society to engage in non-conforming rather than conforming conduct.
>
> R. K. Merton, *Social Theory and Social Structure* (1968)

In some circumstances, the infringement of social codes becomes the 'normal' response — 'expectable' though not culturally approved. Some groups are peculiarly subject to such pressures, leading to high rates of deviance.

Merton identified two important elements in societies such as the USA:
- culturally defined **goals** (e.g. wealth and status) that are held as legitimate objectives for all or most members of the society
- regulatory norms and laws controlling acceptable **means** of reaching for these goals

> Many procedures which from the standpoint of particular individuals would be most efficient in securing desired values — the exercise of force, fraud, power — are ruled out of the institutional area of permitted conduct.
>
> R. K. Merton, *Social Theory and Social Structure* (1968)

Merton made interesting parallels between trying to succeed in society and playing card games, since both involve competition. If people focus on the pleasure of playing the game and are willing to lose, they conform to the rules. If winning is a priority, they are tempted to cheat.

The American dream emphasises career success, with wealth bestowing prestige. The family, school, workplace and media reinforce the need to climb the ladder. Even successful people crave 25% more than they already have. (Note the *synoptic link with media here*.) The message is that any American can succeed with enough effort.

> The cultural manifesto is clear: one must not quit, must not cease striving, must not lessen his goals, for 'not failure, but low aim', is crime.
>
> R. K. Merton, *Social Theory and Social Structure* (1968)

Socialised by this message, people who fail to achieve affluence are more likely to blame their own lack of drive than to recognise the effects of class and racial inequalities. They experience a strain between their aspirations and pressure to abide by laws that regulate the means of reaching the goal. This creates a sense of moral confusion, a particular type of anomie. According to Merton, American culture has a stronger emphasis on achieving goals than on using legal means of reaching them. For example, businessmen who obtain wealth through sharp practice may be admired. In such circumstances, engaging in criminal behaviour is, therefore, common.

> Aberrant behaviour may be regarded sociologically as a symptom of dissociation between culturally prescribed aspirations and socially structured avenues for realising these aspirations.
>
> R. K. Merton, *Social Theory and Social Structure* (1968)

Merton's typology of modes of individual adaptation

Merton therefore implied that society is made unstable by the practical impossibility of all people following the conflicting norms of success and legitimate behaviour. Table 1:1 shows a variety of ways in which people adapt to the situation. Several of these are deviant.

Table 1.1 Merton's typology of modes of individual adaptation

Mode of adaptation	Cultural goals	Institutionalised means
Conformity	Accepted	Accepted
Innovation	Accepted	Rejected
Ritualism	Rejected	Accepted
Retreatism	Rejected	Rejected
Rebellion	Rejected and new goals substituted	Rejected and new means substituted

Conformity

Some people will strive towards the accepted goals and be successful, and will constitute the stable, law-abiding core of society.

Innovation

In this context, innovation is another word for crime. Individuals have such emotional investment in the goal that they are prepared to take risks, especially if their aspirations outweigh their internalisation of moral values. At top economic levels, innovation may involve sharp practice — white-collar or corporate crime that goes unnoticed or unpunished because of the prestige of the offender.

The greatest pressure towards deviation is exerted on lower strata because such people lack access to legitimate means of success. Manual work in the USA is stigmatised with low wages and few opportunities to advance legally. Therefore, crime is more lucrative.

> Despite our persisting open-class ideology, advance towards the success-goal is relatively rare and notably difficult for those armed with little formal education and few economic resources.
>
> R. K. Merton, *Social Theory and Social Structure* (1968)

Poverty in itself does not generate crime, because in some societies lower classes do not share upper-class goals. However, in America, the misleading message is that the majority can be wealthy.

Ritualism

Ritualism involves abandoning or scaling down ambitions because of the difficulty of realising them. Ritualists are, in a way, deviant because they reject the cultural obligation to aspire, preferring the lack of pressure. Their behaviour is 'institutionally permitted though not culturally preferred'. They may cling closely to convention, almost making up in respectability for what they lose in prestige. This is often seen in lower middle-class Americans, who are more likely than the working classes to have been socialised to abide by moral norms.

Retreatism

Retreatism is a rarer adaptation that describes people such as vagrants, alcoholics, drug addicts and psychotics who have mentally dropped out of society. Retreatists may have been initially keen to succeed but could not do so legitimately. They were unable to use illegitimate routes because of internalised prohibitions. To avoid conflict, they abandoned both goals and means and opted for a life '*in* the society but not *of* it'.

US society objects strongly to retreatists — they lack the respectability of conformists and ritualists and the striving of innovators. Their view that prevailing values do not matter threatens the stability of society.

Retreatism is a privatised mode of adaptation. People opting out might gravitate towards centres where there are other deviants and share a subculture but, according to Merton, they are not unified by a new cultural code.

Rebellion

Rebels may be more perceptive than others because they realise the institutional structure is a barrier to the legitimate achievement of goals. They strive for a new order with closer correspondence between merit, effort and reward. Rebel leaders may be members of a rising class, who are successful themselves. They organise the resentful lower strata into a revolutionary group.

Task 1.4

Apply Merton's theory to international athletics. Compare the pressures to succeed with the intrinsic pleasure of the competition and the requirement to keep to the rules. How do some athletes respond to the 'strain' of this situation?

Merton conceded that the strain towards anomie might not affect everyone. There are some people who value non-financial success, such as artistic and academic achievement. However, the outlook for the stability of society is poor when 'calculations of personal advantage and fear of punishment are the only regulatory agencies'.

Children of financially unsuccessful parents are particularly likely to become criminals. Personally disappointed adults compensate by being ambitious for their children, yet the social background underlying the parent's failure is equally likely to hold back the children. Inheriting unrealistic goals, these children will experience strain that can be reduced by 'innovation'.

Merton applied strain theory to various groups of American immigrants. As newcomers, Irish, Jewish and Italian groups experienced pressure to reach financial success. They sometimes achieved this by turning to crime, a famous example being Al Capone. The second generation gained sufficient political power to promote their group's interests and by the third generation many had become successful professionals.

How useful is Merton's theory?

Merton evaluated his own work as follows:
- He acknowledged the need for further research, particularly into the children of failed parents.

- He had not fully explored what predisposes people to one adaptation rather than another.
- Rebellion received little attention.
- He had not put the theory to a full empirical test.
- Herbert Hyman questioned whether people of lower strata all shared mainstream goals. However, what Merton actually said was that *some* were pressurised to reach the wealth goal, not all.

Merton's own summary of how he extended Durkheim's work is useful:

> As initially developed by Durkheim, the concept of anomie referred to a condition of relative normlessness in a society or group…this concept referred to a property of the social and cultural structure, not to a property of individuals confronting that structure. Nevertheless, as the utility of the concept for understanding diverse forms of deviant behaviour became evident, it was extended to refer to a condition of individuals rather than of their environment.
>
> R. K. Merton, *Social Theory and Social Structure* (1968)

Srole and anomie

Anomie is of interest to other sociologists. Leo Srole (1951) suggested that a society is anomic if many of its members feel that:
- community leaders are indifferent to one's needs
- little can be accomplished in the society, which is unpredictable and lacks order
- life-goals are receding rather than being realised
- there is a sense of futility
- one cannot count on personal associates for social and psychological support

Task 1.5

Which of Srole's indicators would justify describing present-day Iraq as anomic? Which adaptations from Merton's list would you expect to find there?

Kingsley Davis: how prostitution is functional

In an essay entitled 'Sexual behaviour' (1961), functionalist Kingsley Davis echoed Durkheim's view that deviance is inevitable and even performs necessary functions in society. He maintained that it was impossible to imagine a social system without prostitution. First, it would require the absence of marriage and equivalent relationships in which exclusiveness, jealousy of potential rivals and long-term commitment are important features. Second, it would require all sexual desire to be mutually complementary, so that everyone found willing partners.

In reality, all developed societies attempt to contain people's sexual urges to preserve social order, control procreation and socialise children. Prostitution acts as a safety valve, allowing some to seek sexual variety surreptitiously without compromising their marriages. Likewise, there will always be relatively unattractive people unable to find sexual partners unless they pay for their services.

While males remain the economically dominant sex, it will be more common for men to use women for prostitution than for women to use men. Working-class women are drawn into prostitution when it pays better than the unskilled work they might otherwise do, although the stigma acts as a disincentive. The number of prostitutes has declined as women's pay has drawn closer to that of men and changing sexual morality means that sexual desire can be satisfied without the commitment of marriage. Nevertheless, 'the oldest profession in the world' performs an indispensable function.

Task 1.6

Like Durkheim and Davis, Marshall Clinard (*Sociology and Deviant Behaviour, 1974*) claimed that some forms of deviance are useful, without being desirable. This is because they draw attention to defects in society or in organisations that need to be addressed.

Suggest possible reasons for the following examples of deviance and improvements that might be made in the relevant organisations:

- an exceptionally high rate of (apparent) suicides amongst young soldiers at Deepcut barracks in Surrey
- disproportionate expulsion of black male students from British schools
- high rates of industrial sabotage (deliberate damage by employees) at places of work

Control theory

Other sociologists have followed Durkheim in viewing deviance as resulting from an absence of social control and suggesting that a reduction in control or 'containment' will generate further deviance by allowing people to follow their 'natural' inclinations. Among these are control theorists and New Right theorists. The sometimes contradictory views of the New Right are covered in Chapter 7.

Despite their differences, Durkheim and Merton both suggested that the prevailing values in western societies are acceptable to most people and, although there may be too much pressure for financial success and some laws may become outdated, the system does not need to be fundamentally challenged.

A more recent supporter of this **consensus** position is the American control theorist Travis Hirschi. In *Causes of Delinquency* (written in 1969, revised in 2002) he addressed the interesting question of what makes people *conform* — in other words, what controls them when it might be easier to reach material goals through crime. This is a different angle from Merton, who asked why people *deviate*. Hirschi suggested four influences that act as controls, drawing on evidence from young people:

- **Attachment** Those who have close bonds with parents, teachers and significant others are reluctant to disappoint them. 'If a person does not care about the wishes and expectations of other people…if he is insensitive to the opinion of others, then he is to that extent not bound by the norms.' The effects of attachment are the same in all classes of the population, even if the youth is attached to people who are themselves delinquent, 'as all accept conventional patterns of conduct as ultimately desirable'.

- **Commitment** People committed to a good education and career are less likely to deviate because it would damage their reputations and interfere with their progress. Adolescents who express little desire to do well at school or to achieve in other activities commit more delinquent acts.

- **Involvement** People busy studying or working lack the time for deviant activities. Delinquency occurs mainly among those who have left school at the minimum age and do not yet have family breadwinner responsibilities. Hirschi's respondents who described themselves as bored with adolescence were more likely to admit to offences and to have police records than those who spent time on homework and hobbies.

- **Belief** Those with weak beliefs in the moral validity of social rules are more likely to deviate. Hirschi claimed that there were no substantial classes or subcultures in American society that positively encouraged crime or were even neutral about it. Delinquents may well believe that deviant acts are wrong, but, if other controlling forces are absent, their beliefs may not be strong enough to make them conform.

Hirschi found that there was often a correlation between these factors. A person closely attached to conventional people was more likely to be committed and involved in conventional activities, and to accept prevailing beliefs. Students performing poorly academically tended to reject teachers' authority, have weak ties with their parents and be delinquent. Boys doing well at school, and who were close to their fathers, tended not to have delinquent friends; if they did, they were unlikely to be unduly influenced by them. Notice that Hirschi's factors make *synoptic links between deviance and other topics such as family, education, work and leisure, and religion (beliefs)*.

While Merton suggested that aspirations often tempt people into crime, Hirschi found the opposite. Young people who did not want to go to college had committed more delinquent acts than those who hoped to go. Hirschi's sample had few examples of keen working-class or ethnic-minority students unable to afford college — in other words, there was little evidence of strain. However, among those young people that he surveyed, ambition generated conformity, not deviance.

Hirschi's research was based on detailed questionnaires given to over 4000 high school students (both boys and girls), school records of their achievement and police data on the boys in the sample. Apparently, he assumed that all delinquents are male!

His conclusions tend to rest on correlations between different aspects of boys' behaviour and attitudes. However, remarks about 'men' and 'individuals' suggest that his theories are intended to apply to adults and to both sexes. Feminists' criticise such 'malestream' sociology.

Hirschi did acknowledge one research limitation. He wished he had included more questions about the influence of delinquent friends and he recommended further research into the effects of delinquent activities on self-concept and self-esteem. His ideas have been interpreted as suggesting that if individuals are not bonded to society, governments need to encourage integration to reduce the likelihood of deviance. However, Marxists reject the implication that people are naturally inclined to commit crime.

Summary

- Crime is behaviour that breaks the laws of a society.
- Deviance is behaviour that differs from the norms of a particular group or society.
- Social constructionists, Marxists, functionalists and feminists strongly disagree about the definitions and causes of crime and deviance.
- Consensus theorists such as Durkheim believe that people need to be socialised to accept majority values and the law, because social order benefits all.
- A little deviance is inevitable and even functional, but a lot implies that society is insufficiently integrated. Lack of agreement over norms is called anomie.
- Merton's strain theory developed the notion of anomie as a mismatch between people's goals and the existence of socially approved means to reach them.

- Davis followed Durkheim in exploring the social function of types of deviance such as prostitution.
- Hirschi's version of **control theory** contrasts with Merton by exploring not why people deviate but the **bonds** that discourage deviation.
- Merton and Hirschi disagreed about whether ambitions encourage deviance or conformity.

Task 1.7

Assess the usefulness of consensus approaches such as functionalism in explaining the causes and extent of deviance in society.

Guidance

Begin by defining a consensus approach, relating it to the functionalist view of the need for social solidarity through shared values.

For *knowledge* marks, explain the views of Durkheim, Merton and Davis, using key vocabulary and covering both causes and extent. Hirschi could be discussed by arguing that lack of bonds causes crime. After reading on, you will be able to incorporate the consensus views of the New Right.

For *assessment* marks, discuss:

- the usefulness of Durkheim's work as a basis for later researchers to develop
- the researchers' own comments on their work
- specific situations to which their views can be applied (briefly)
- relevant similarities and differences between them
- after further reading, how Marxists and social constructionists would disagree on the key issues

In *conclusion*, sum up the value and limitations of consensus approaches to deviance.

Useful websites

- Crime and deviance section of Dave Harris's site (Focus on: Social disorganisation/social strain theories)
  www.arasite.org/socdis.html
- Sociology site of Hewett School, Norfolk (Focus on: Durkheim's anomie)
  www.hewett.norfolk.sch.uk/CURRIC/soc/crime/anomie.htm

Further reading

- Croall, H. (1998) *Crime and Society in Britain*, Pearson Education.
- Moore, S. (1996) *Investigating Crime and Deviance*, Collins.
- Clinard, M. (1974) *Sociology and Deviant Behaviour*, Holt, Rinehart and Winston (New York).

Chapter 2

How do Marxists explain crime?

Core Marxist beliefs about crime

Traditional Marxists disagree with consensus theorists about who makes laws, who benefits from social control and why crime occurs. They view most societies as being in a state of class conflict and suggest the following:

- Laws are made by the bourgeoisie (ruling class), largely to protect their own interests. They decide what constitutes crime and use the police and courts as agents of social control to maintain their dominant position. Institutions such as the family, the education system and religious bodies socialise people to respect private property and hierarchy, discouraging revolution.
- Attempts by the proletariat (working class) to gain a fairer share of goods are called property crimes. They are publicised by the media and are punished severely. Similarly, acts that express alienation from capitalism, such as vandalism, graffiti and violence, are targeted by police in frequent patrols of working-class areas.
- Capitalism breeds competitiveness and commodity fetishism, a situation in which material possessions are held in high esteem. Wealthy owners of businesses, who lack the justification of the relatively poor, commit corporate crime to increase their wealth even more. These offences, which range from financial swindles to ruthless attempts to increase company profits by ignoring safety and environmental regulations, involve greater sums of money and more ruined lives than street crimes by the working class. Yet, in general, such offences are not regarded as the province of the police and criminal courts. They often go unpunished or are dealt with more leniently by health and safety officials or specialist courts, and receive less media coverage. Likewise, the white-collar crimes of professionals are less likely to be dealt with by the criminal justice system than are offences by the working class.
- In communist societies, there would be no need for crime.

Steven Box: crime of the powerful

These Marxist ideas were explored by Steven Box in *Power, Crime and Mystification* (1983). His aim was to demonstrate that, although the mass media foster public fears of working-class disorder and street crime, the reality is different.

> People in powerful positions will do, and have done, some pretty dreadful things. Unfortunately, this is all lost to those who concentrate entirely on crimes committed by the powerless...Crimes of the powerful can only be ignored at the risk of enormously increasing our chances of being victimised by them.
>
> S. Box, *Power, Crime and Mystification* (1983)

Box noted that most people convicted of serious offences are young uneducated males, often unemployed, who live in impoverished neighbourhoods and frequently belong to ethnic minorities. Street crimes such as robbery, assault and vandalism may well be increasing as the material conditions of these groups deteriorate. Nevertheless, this is only *'a* crime problem and not *the* crime problem'. Their victims' sufferings undoubtedly need to be addressed, but there is a danger of our attention being distracted from the larger-scale crimes of upper- and middle-class criminals.

Self-report and victimisation surveys reveal that a higher proportion of crimes are committed by white, well-educated females and by older people than official statistics suggest. Police figures are distorted by a number of factors, which are explored in Task 2.1.

Task 2.1

Box's ideas of the strategies used by the criminal justice system are summarised in the table below. Study the table and then discuss the questions that follow.

Strategy	Explanation or example
Differential deployment	'For example, swamping certain parts of London where the West Indian population is prominent'
Methodological suspicion	'Routinely suspecting only a limited proportion of the population, particularly those with criminal records or known criminal associates'
Plea-bargaining	Negotiating a guilty plea in return for being charged with a less serious offence
Judicial decisions	'...which take as much notice of who you are as they do of what you have apparently done'

Task 2.1 (continued)

(a) As a Marxist, Box perceived the proletariat as being criminalised by these strategies. How might some of these strategies be justified by people with a different perspective?

(b) Which of Box's points could be easily checked by another researcher? Are any of them likely to be subjective (opinion based)?

Guidance

- Considerations of limited police time and manpower could inform your first answer.
- Raising questions about the **reliability** and **validity** of Box's evidence would be likely to gain evaluation marks in an essay.

Box argued that members of the proletariat, once they have been stigmatised by the discriminatory criminal justice system, find it even harder to gain employment. Therefore, either out of desperation or a sense of injustice, they may become hardened criminals and spend long periods of their lives in prison. The increased threat they pose confirms public fears of this group, justifying the attention they receive from the agents of social control. The vicious circle of suspicion and escalating offending that he described has much in common with the labelling theory of crime, explored in Chapter 3.

Task 2.2

Read the passage and answer the question that follows.

According to the Home Office website, 'Antisocial Behaviour Orders (ASBOs) are statutory measures that aim to protect the public from behaviour that…is likely to cause harassment, alarm or distress'. Local authorities, police and social landlords can apply for an order against the alleged offender. Decisions can be based on hearsay and witness evidence from the public without the delay of a court trial. People can be banned from an area or from associating with named others for 2 years and can be arrested if the order is breached.

People have received ASBOs for vandalism, abusive behaviour, violence, harassmen, fly posting, animal rights protests, demonstrating against the sale of bulldozers to Israel, campaigning against council 'corruption' and attempting suicide in public places.

A MORI opinion poll published in 2005 claimed that 82% of the British public were in favour of ASBOs. However, only 39% believed they were effective in their current form.

Task 2.2 (continued)

Question

What would Marxists think of ASBOs?

Guidance

How many of the actions mentioned above could be viewed as being against capitalist interests?

Does the public popularity of the orders prove that ASBOs protect ordinary people or could this be a case of **false consciousness** (being misled by capitalist ideology)?

Box argued cleverly with anti-Marxist critics. Consider the Marxist position that criminal legislation predominantly benefits the bourgeoisie. One criticism of this is that much legislation, such as regulations concerning health and safety at work, benefits the proletariat. Box's view is that some laws safeguard the interests of less powerful groups 'basically, to keep them quiet' and that such legislation is often ineffectually enforced. A further critcism is that everyone, not just the powerful, feels safer as a result of laws against murder, rape, arson, robbery, theft and assault. Box agreed that this is true but said that these terms are narrowly defined by the powerful. If the terms are more broadly defined, the proletariat are more vulnerable to crimes of this general nature.

Box argued that only some kinds of avoidable killing are defined as murder. He cited evidence for deaths excluded from this definition resulting from:

- negligence, such as an employer's failure to maintain safe working conditions
- reluctance of governmental agencies to focus on environmental health risks
- pharmaceutical companies bribing health authorities to approve dangerous drugs or marketing inadequately tested drugs aggressively
- failure of car manufacturers to recall defective vehicles, in order to avoid financial loss

We are encouraged to see murder as a particular act involving a very limited range of stereotypical actors, instruments, situations and motives.

S. Box, *Power, Crime and Mystification* (1983)

Box cited parallel situations for other crimes:

- Theft — a worker taking money from a till is theft, whereas a boss reducing an employee's wages is 'the labour market operating reasonably'

- Rape — powerful bosses are more likely to be able to force themselves on female employees without being accused of rape than powerless men committing the same act
- Assault — this should include verbal assaults that break people's spirit, control of the mentally ill by drugs and governments bombing civilians, but it is much more narrowly defined

Task 2.3

Can you think of a ruling class or state version of arson (illegally setting things on fire)?

Guidance

Search the internet using the words 'napalm Vietnam'.

Box argued that criminal laws 'do not protect the less powerful from being killed, sexually exploited, deprived of what little property they possess, or being physically and psychologically damaged through the greed, apathy, negligence, indifference, and the unaccountability of the relatively more powerful'.

Definitions of crime change over time, but this should not be taken, as Durkheim suggests, to imply a value consensus. Though laws change, most continue to reflect bourgeois interests. The UK government appears to act as a neutral referee between interest groups by consulting those likely to be affected in the course of producing new legislation. Parliamentary debates suggest all views are being heard and voted upon. However, as there are no radically left-wing parties, the agenda is already set; changes that Marxists might approve are never suggested. The ruling class remains in control and steers public opinion through hegemony, the control of ideas, through their manipulation of capitalist-controlled media and institutions such as schools.

Therefore, Box argued, most people accept the 'official view' of crime, being sensitised to muggers, football hooligans, housebreakers, terrorists and 'scroungers' because their acts are well publicised. In contrast, reports of factory inspectorates and specialist judicial agencies are rarely heard, so few people are aware of crimes committed by corporate managers against stockholders, employees and consumers.

Those in powerful positions are able to 'mystify' the public. Crimes of governments, such as the victimisation of less economically developed countries, and crimes of control agents, such as police and prison officers assaulting or using deadly force against suspects and prisoners, are frequently hidden. Box devoted a chapter to police-caused homicides and corruption. He drew on UK and US secondary sources to suggest that these offences are rife but are usually overlooked by governments that allow the police themselves to investigate public complaints. Governments need police to quell riots and other forms of working-class resistance. However, this is a difficult and dangerous task and the police are themselves frequently working class. Box argued, highly controversially, that in return for performing their essential role in maintaining social order 'they are allowed to go beyond the limits of the law'.

Task 2.4

Several of the cases below were cited by Box as examples of 'police brutality'. Box suggested that victims of police-caused homicides are not randomly distributed but are 'drawn from the economically marginalised, politically radical and ethnically oppressed'. Which of the examples below might support his theory?

- In 1979, according to eyewitnesses, Blair Peach, a socialist special-school teacher from New Zealand, died after being hit by police when he was leaving a legal demonstration against the National Front.
- In 1981, Winston Rose (black, aged 27), died in a police van after being restrained by 11 police officers taking him to a psychiatric hospital.
- In 2000, Asif Dad, 26, died in the custody of Essex police. According to the police, Dad was arrested after they were called to a street disturbance and he collapsed and died after a struggle.
- In 2001, Derek Bennett (black, age unknown) was shot dead in the street by Brixton police who alleged they were called by a member of the public. Bennett was carrying a novelty lighter shaped like a gun.
- In 2002, Harry Stanley, 46, a Scottish decorator, was shot dead by police who thought he had a shotgun. He was carrying a table leg wrapped in a plastic bag.
- In 2005, Jean Charles de Menezes, 27, a Brazilian electrician working in London, was shot dead by police who mistook him for one of the suicide bombers targeting the capital.

What is corporate crime?

A corporate crime is defined as an illegal act of omission or commission by members of a legitimate organisation to increase its profits or influence. Such acts have a serious physical or economic impact on employees, consumers, the general public, other corporations and organisations. Though profit-making companies are the main focus, harmful acts of governments are sometimes included.

Corporate crime is rendered invisible for the following reasons:
- Its planning and execution is sophisticated and complex — for example, corporate tax evasion and price fixing.
- People are often unaware of being victims. The effects can be long term — for example, industrial diseases and air pollution.
- Legal restrictions are non-existent or weak. Instead of the police, inspectorates and government departments attempt to regulate corporations. Punishments, when imposed, are usually fines, which do not have much deterrent effect. Those found guilty are less likely to lose their jobs or experience social stigma than are conventional criminals.
- It is easy for those with respectable identities to deny knowledge or personal responsibility for corporate crimes, claiming accident rather than intention or that they have caused little personal suffering — for example, tax evasion, where government revenue only is affected.
- It is under-reported by the popular media.
- It has been neglected by many sociologists, who have focused more on street crime.

Capitalist definitions of serious crime are ideological constructs. They act as strategies of social control of the working class, distracting attention from corporate and state crimes in the following ways:
- They render underprivileged people more likely to be arrested, convicted and imprisoned, even though the amount of personal damage and injury they cause may be less than that caused by powerful offenders.
- They create the illusion that the 'dangerous' classes are located at the bottom of various hierarchies and that such people are morally inferior, deserving both poverty and punishment.
- They render invisible the harm and deprivation imposed on ordinary people by states, and by transnational and other corporations. Though governments and TNCs create poor conditions that generate working-class crime, locally and globally, such crime is instead attributed to individual pathology (abnormality) or to the influence of neighbourhoods and subcultures. (Global crime issues are further explored in Chapter 5.)
- They give the impression that everyone is treated equally by the criminal justice system.
- They make ordinary people depend on the state to combat crime, even though the state and its agents victimise ordinary people.

Many studies of corporate crime have been carried out in the USA. Some of the better-known studies are listed in Box 2.1 These could be followed up through wider reading.

Box 2.1
Corporate crime studies in the USA

Richard Quinney, *The Social Reality of Crime* (1970)

Quinney's approach is both Marxist and social constructionist: 'Without the concept of crime, crime would not exist as a phenomenon…the conceptions are important because of their consequences'. The public accept the 'reality' of crime constructed by the ruling classes and grant them authority that maintains their power. Governments frequently organise commissions investigating particular types of crime, to appear to be taking action. However, they only implement recommendations that suit them. Anti-crime programmes often reduce civil liberties, such as the 'preventive detention' of criminal suspects without trial. Quinney's comments on police powers resemble Box's.

> Increased use of police power has been justified as necessary to combat civil disorder. But the paradox is that the violence that the police attempt to control is inspired in many instances by the police themselves. And more important, much of the violence is actually committed by the police…So it is that looting of property during race 'riots' is defined as violence…but the killing of looters is legitimate…Let us hope that the war on crime will not be won if it means the further legitimisation of state violence and the denial of individual freedom.

Frank Pearce, *Crimes of the Powerful* (1976)

Pearce's examples of the links between organised crime, American businesses and governments now seem outdated, but his general points are important. He notes the promotion of the **individualistic ideology** — the view that crime is committed by abnormal people. If, instead, the public realised that crime stems from class inequalities, they would be keener to support radical movements. The occasional implementation of laws disadvantaging the rich gives the impression that the state is neutral.

Laureen Snider, 'The politics of crime control', in F. Pearce and M. Woodiwiss, (eds) *Global Crime Connections* (1993)

Street crime in the USA costs $4 billion dollars a year, whereas corporate crime costs more than 20 times this amount.

The USA has the highest murder rate in the developed world: 20 000 murders a year. This is paralleled by 14 000 deaths through industrial accidents, 30 000 from unsafe consumer products and hundreds of thousands of cancer deaths caused by environmental pollution, both legal and illegal.

Countless injuries and occupation-induced illnesses are due to employer negligence and are, therefore, avoidable.

Industrial capitalism depends on the exploitation of human and natural resources, using them in the cheapest possible fashion to extract the maximum return. Therefore, the future prospects for caring treatment of employees and sustainable development are poor.

History does not allow us to view this scenario optimistically, despite the fact that the survival of our species is ultimately at stake.

William Chambliss, *Power, Politics and Crime* (1999)

Law enforcement agencies target wage labourers and ethnic minorities as inherently criminal, while hiding the corruption of governments, corporations and their own staff. This results in:

- an alienated proletariat, who view the law as an instrument of oppression
- cynical middle classes accepting corruption as normal
- office holders using power for personal gain

How widespread is corporate crime in Britain?

Gary Slapper and Steve Tombs in *Corporate Crime* (1999) suggest there has been insufficient British research into this problem. Analysing the reasons for this provides a *synoptic link with research methods*.

- It is hard to study such crime through ethnography, because gaining access to the boardroom is less likely than being able to observe working-class offenders.
- Secondary sources such as business records, minutes and memos are kept secure.
- Well-educated individuals, with polished social skills, are unlikely to speak unguardedly.
- If a violation is being investigated, company members are unlikely to be available for interview.
- Small businesses are difficult to investigate as they may not even be registered.
- Researchers may have to rely on the testimonies of investigative journalists and whistleblowers, casting doubt on the reliability and representativeness of the findings.

Slapper and Tombs differ from those Marxists who argue that street crime dominates the media because they do acknowledge that some types of corporate crime hit the headlines. The creation of the Serious Fraud Office in 1987 reflected government determination to reduce major financial swindles — unsurprisingly, because they undermine consumer confidence in investments, upon which capitalism depends.

However, other types of corporate crime, relating to the health and safety of workers and the safeguarding of the environment, are less likely to be reported because they are poorly regulated. Preventing such offences would involve regular scrutiny of the minute details of production, a move deemed to interfere with free enterprise. Deregulation in these areas is in the interests of capitalism and the public are led to believe that what is good for business is good for employees. Slapper and Tombs find this situation deplorable because those most likely to suffer from dangerous working conditions and unhealthy environments are the poorest people, who are the least able to articulate their rights.

Task 2.5

Assess the extent to which the following evidence echoes the views of Slapper and Tombs.

Exploitation of 1 million UK workers exposed

The UK government must implement international labour standards, if the exploitation of Britain's 1 million homeworkers is to be halted. That is the finding of a new report — *Made at Home* — published today by Oxfam, the TUC and the NGH (National Group on Homeworking).

Women workers around the world who produce goods sold in Britain's have no minimum wage, no sick pay, no maternity leave, no redundancy pay, forced overtime and no checks on health and safety. However, it is also the story of many British workers supplying the same supermarkets and retailers.

The main problem is that homeworkers are often isolated, without the support of workmates or a union to speak up for them. Many are not 'employees' and so lack even the most basic employment rights, including protection against unfair dismissal and maternity leave.

Legally, all homeworkers should be getting the minimum wage and holiday pay, but the reality is that many employers prey upon and exploit their vulnerable position…If they complain, it is likely that their supply of work will stop without notice, so many homeworkers stay silent and abuses go unreported.

Extracts from Oxfam GB press release, 17 May 2004

What is white-collar crime?

Though not a Marxist, American Edwin Sutherland, in his influential book *White Collar Crime* (1949), was one of the first sociologists to draw attention to the prevalence of this type of crime. He defined it as 'crime committed by a person of respectability and high status in the course of his occupation'.

If his definition sounds masculine, this reflects the time in which it was written. Some sociologists, including Sutherland, tend to blur the boundaries between white-collar crime and corporate crime. Others use the terms 'white-collar crime' or 'occupational crime' to refer to acts committed by individuals for their own benefit as opposed to that of the company. A white-collar crime might be a single small act of theft, embezzlement or bribery, or a long-term 'scam', such as regularly taking home company property.

The distinction between personal and company profit is complicated when the perpetrator is the owner or a major shareholder of the company and will benefit directly from its increased profits. This was the case with Robert Maxwell, the late proprietor of Mirror Group newspapers. The millionaire used his power to persuade three directors of Bishopsgate Investment Management, the company managing his employees' pension funds, to sign over money so that he could buy shares in his other public companies. He then used the shares as collateral for bank loans. He broke the law by not replacing the money in the pension funds. When his business empire collapsed, 30 000 employees found that they had lost their pension fund, which totalled £43 million.

This complicated situation was handled by the Serious Fraud Office. Two of Maxwell's sons, who both held high positions in the Maxwell Group and inherited the remnants of the business after their father's death, eventually convinced the court that they had not been involved in a conspiracy to defraud company pensioners.

Sutherland argued that the financial losses from white-collar crime, great as they are, are less important than the damage to social relations. Ordinary people rely on being able to pay into pension schemes throughout their working lives, secure in the knowledge that they will have money to live on after retirement. While street crimes produce little effect on social institutions, white-collar and corporate crimes can destroy trust in important institutions and hence produce greater social disorganisation.

Are Marxists idealists?

Jock Young described Marxism as 'left idealism'. An American publication by Richard Quinney and John Wildeman, entitled *The Problem of Crime: A Peace and Social Justice Perspective* (1991) might be regarded as idealistic. Marx rejected religion as 'the opium of the people', arguing that it persuaded people to accept poverty and oppression in the hope of being rewarded in the afterlife. In contrast, Quinney has combined the Marxist ideas and abhorrence of state violence expressed in his earlier work with eastern spirituality to suggest a new direction for 'non-violent criminology'.

Rather than attempting to create a good society first and then trying to make ourselves better human beings, we have to work on the two simultaneously.

He advocates seeking inner peace through spiritual enlightenment, arguing that this will produce compassion and social justice, eliminating the motivation for crime and the violent suppression of crime.

Criminologists should turn from gathering data on how best to control offenders and instead seek answers to the question: 'What is lacking in the lives of our fellows that gives them no alternative but a life of crime and violence?'

Practical measures he advocates in his peace and social justice programme include:

- expansion of physical and mental health services for high-risk youths and their parents
- high-quality early education for children at risk
- family support programmes to minimise domestic violence and child abuse
- consistently supportive services for young offenders
- non-punitive treatment for drug abuse
- mediation between victims, offenders and their parents, with offenders restoring what was lost to the victim (restorative justice) and being rehabilitated into society
- the abolition of the death penalty, which repays violence with violence

Despite its somewhat mystical language, Quinney and Wildeman's book retains central Marxist ideas. Together with the recent works of Chambliss, and Slapper and Tombs, it shows that traditional Marxism remains a significant influence on both sides of the Atlantic, even though left-wing theories have developed in other directions.

Task 2.6

Identify and briefly explain three criticisms of Marxist theories of crime. (12 marks)

Guidance

- Write each criticism as a separate paragraph, starting with a key phrase and then expanding upon it. You could select some of the criticisms discussed by Steven Box (above), refer to Slapper and Tombs's evidence of government concern over corporate crime or expand on the idea that Marxists are too idealistic and 'soft' on working-class crime' (Quinney and Wildeman).
- Evidence of crime in the former USSR and communist China could be used to undermine the view that capitalism causes crime. Some types of crime have little connection with economic systems.
- There is a contradiction between Marxist claims that agents of social control unreasonably target the proletariat and Marxist attempts to justify working-class crime because of structural inequalities.

Task 2.6 (continued)

- Consensus theories could be offered as an alternative to Marxist explanations for crime.
- Criticisms can be positive, so you could cite evidence supporting a particular aspect of Marxist theory.

Summary

- Marxists view society as divided by class. Laws are made by the bourgeoisie to protect their own interests.
- Proletarian acts to gain a fairer share of goods or that express alienation from capitalism are called crimes and are targeted by police.
- Capitalism breeds competitiveness, tempting wealthy people to commit corporate and white-collar crime. These offences involve greater sums of money and ruin more lives than working-class street crimes, yet receive less attention and lighter punishments.
- In a communist society there would be no need for crime.
- Box argues that offences that have working-class victims are often not viewed officially as crimes, which renders them invisible. He cites examples of crimes by the powerful, including the police, transnational companies and governments.
- Quinney, Pearce, Snider and Chambliss provide evidence of widespread and damaging corporate crime in the USA.
- Slapper and Tombs explore similar areas in Britain. They identify methodological problems of researching corporate crime and the lack of attention to crimes that threaten health and safety, and the environment.
- Quinney and Wildeman's peace and social justice perspective provides a contrast to the anti-religious outlook of many Marxists.

Useful websites

- Institute of Race Relations: Black Deaths in Custody
  www.irr.org.uk/2002/november/ak000006.html
- Indymedia UK (radical views on ASBOs and other aspects of social control)
  www.indymedia.org.uk/en/2004/08/296676.html
- Serious Fraud Office
  www.sfo.gov.uk/

Further reading

- Box, S. (1983) *Power, Crime and Mystification*, Tavistock Publications.
- Hall, S. et al. (1978) *Policing the Crisis: Mugging, the State, and Law and Order*, Macmillan Press.
- Slapper, G. and Tombs, S. (1999) *Corporate Crime*, Pearson.

Social constructionist theories

Functionalists and Marxists take a structuralist approach to the study of crime and deviance, focusing on large groups such as social classes; social constructionists or interactionists are more interested in examining the reasons why individuals become labelled as deviant and how social responses to them may amplify deviance. They investigate these areas by participant observation, interviews with small groups and analysis of media coverage. This chapter has useful *synoptic links with methods and media*.

Why is deviance viewed as a social construction?

Chapter 1 referred briefly to Howard Becker's view that deviance is a social construction. In the highly influential study *Outsiders* (1963), Becker suggested that laymen ask the wrong questions about deviance. They want to know: 'Why do they do it? What is there about them that leads them to do forbidden things?'

Assumptions are made that there is something qualitatively distinct about acts that break social rules and about the people who commit them. The values of the group making the judgement are generally accepted.

Yet different groups regard different acts as deviant — for example, world religions differ in their food taboos. This, therefore, should alert us to the possibility that deviance is not an *objective* fact but is a *subjective* (opinion-based) phenomenon that depends on particular people making judgements in particular situations.

Becker examined different uses of the word 'deviance':
- anything that differs from what is most common (deviation from the mean)
- pathological ('sick') behaviour, suggesting the person is failing to function well within the 'body' of society, for example by exhibiting signs of mental illness or relating poorly to others
- failure to obey society's formal or informal rules

Becker found this third interpretation the most relevant. However, he noted that society's rules are hard to identify because any society has many groups, each with its own set of rules. Abiding by the rules of one group may mean breaking the rules of another.

Task 3.1

Think of ways in which the following people would find it difficult to conform to the expectations (informal rules) of other members of society:

- an Orthodox Jew
- a vegan
- a person with little income
- someone with literacy problems
- a Rastafarian

Note: Ganja (marijuana) is considered to be the 'wisdom weed' by Rastafarians, because they believe that its use helps people to gain wisdom. The smoking of ganja is a part of a religious ritual. When there is a large gathering of Rastafarians, a chalice, which is a large pipe for smoking, may be passed around and smoked. This is similar to the passing around of a communion cup (also called a chalice) by some Christian denominations.

Adapted from The Afrocentric Experience website www.swagga.com/ganga.htm

Rastafarians smoking ganja (marijuana)

Task 3.1 illustrates Becker's main thesis that acts are not deviant in themselves. Otherwise, how could the use of marijuana be conformist in a Rastafarian gathering and deviant in 'respectable' non-Rastafarian settings?

The following quotation is important enough to memorise, at least in part.

> Social groups create deviance by making the rules whose infraction constitutes deviance, and by applying those rules to particular people and labelling them as outsiders. From this point of view, deviance is not a quality of the act the person commits, but rather a consequence of the application by others of rules and sanctions to an 'offender'. The deviant is one to whom that label has successfully been applied; deviant behaviour is behaviour that people so label.
>
> H. Becker, *Outsiders* (1963)

Labelling is the public application of a negative description, such as 'deviant' or 'offender', to a relatively powerless individual. Becker argued that researchers cannot expect to find common factors of personality or life situations that will explain deviance because some people are wrongly labelled as deviant and some rule breakers escape notice. This is conveyed by his four-cell formulation, shown in Table 3.1.

Table 3.1 Becker's four-cell formulation

Perception by significant others:	Obedient behaviour	Rule-breaking behaviour
Perceived as deviant	Falsely accused	Pure deviant
Not perceived as deviant	Conforming	Secret deviant

Task 3.2

(a) Think of a situation in which all members of a group may be assumed to be deviant, even though only some have broken a rule.

(b) Suggest two reasons why some people who have broken a rule are not labelled as deviant.

Becker suggested that in the case of stigmatised sexual behaviour, individuals may escape labelling if they are discreet in their activities, allowing others to 'turn a blind eye'. However, if deviants 'come out', and make public statements about their lifestyles, figures in authority feel obliged to condemn the acts as unacceptable. You may recall that Charles Kennedy felt it necessary to resign as leader of the Liberal Democrat Party soon after he had formally announced his alcohol problem, even though it was already public knowledge.

The degree to which people respond to an act as deviant also depends on:

- whether there is a 'drive' against the type of act at the time — thus, an act receives more negative attention if it relates to contemporary moral panic (an exaggerated fear of a particular type of behaviour, usually whipped up by the media)

- how much harm is done — reckless behaviour is more likely to be condemned when it results in serious damage, even though the outcome is often a matter of chance
- who commits the act and the identity of the victim — acts are more likely to be pronounced deviant if the perpetrator is low status and the victim is high status

Becker related status to class, age, gender and ethnicity, which contrasts with Marxists, who focus mainly on class. Thus, Marxists would agree that corporate crime is less likely to be labelled because of the class of the perpetrator, but would be less interested in reasons why a promiscuous girl might receive more censure than a boy 'sowing wild oats'.

Becker's view was as radical as Marxism in drawing attention to the large number of deviants who remain unsuspected or unrevealed because of their power. Although not all members of society agree about what the rules should be, the most powerful impose their choice on others and label subsequent rule-breakers as deviant.

How do people come to view themselves as outsiders?

Becker disagreed with positivist sociologists who carried out multivariate analysis on the backgrounds of offenders and suggested that criminal behaviour can be predicted when there is a combination of traits such as low intelligence and a 'broken home'. He argued that deviant patterns of behaviour develop in an orderly sequence. Predisposing factors that might, in other circumstances, lead someone to deviate, will not do so if the key situations do not arise. The steps Becker identified are as follows:

1 **Commission of a nonconforming act** (primary deviation) This may be unintentional if the person is deeply involved in a subculture and is unaware of mainstream rules. It could be an act of impulse committed by a person insufficiently committed to conventional society to feel obliged to follow its norms, such as a person with neither a job nor dependents. (This particular point resembles Hirschi's control theory.)
2 **Being caught in the deviant act and publicly identified** This may well depend on the social status of the person.
3 **Being labelled as deviant in general** Although the person may only have committed one deviant act, the reputation for being the kind of person who

breaks moral rules may lead to rejection from conventional groups — for example, losing a job.

4 **Learning to enjoy the deviance** Once isolated from conventional circles, the individual may seek out similar deviants and become immersed in a subculture of experienced deviants, such as a group of habitual drug takers or thieves. This provides more varied opportunities because the group offers advice on how to perform the deviant act more successfully and how to reduce the risks of being caught. The person may learn the group's self-justifying rationale or ideology and repress any doubts about the act, which is normal within the group. Becoming more committed confirms the person's deviant **self-identity**. Others will view the person as having master status as a deviant, with the deviant behaviour being the defining characteristic.

5 **Secondary deviance** Now unable to sustain a legitimate career, the deviant may drift into new areas of more serious deviance, such as committing crime for financial survival or retreating into addiction.

6 **Deviant career** By now it has become unlikely that the outsider will be able to regain a law abiding reputation. The initial labelling has resulted in a self-fulfilling prophecy. The prediction that the person was likely to deviate again became true.

> The treatment of deviants denies them the ordinary means of carrying on the routines of everyday life open to most people. Because of this denial, the deviant must of necessity develop illegitimate routines.
>
> H. Becker, *Outsiders* (1963)

Becker's theory has been criticised as too deterministic, but this is not the case. His comments below could be quoted for *evaluation* marks in an essay.

> Obviously everyone caught in one deviant act and labelled a deviant does not move inevitably towards greater deviance in the way the preceding remarks might suggest. The prophecies do not always confirm themselves; the mechanisms do not always work.
>
> H. Becker, *Outsiders* (1963)

Becker cited research by Reiss (1961) into juvenile boys acting as prostitutes to adult homosexuals. These boys rarely graduated to the secondary deviance of becoming active homosexuals because:

- if arrested, as minors they were viewed as victims, even though they were the exploiters
- they regarded the act as a means of making money, not as a preferred lifestyle
- their group forbade the formation of relationships with adult customers

Thus, they did not acquire public identity or self-identity as practising homosexuals.

In contrast, cured drug addicts may be regarded by others as being still addicted, making it difficult for them to be accepted back into conventional roles.

Becker also researched pop musicians as a deviant occupational group. Life on the road and working unsocial hours increasingly cut them off from other types of people. Additionally, as performers they were expected to dress and behave unconventionally, take drugs and speak a group argot (a distinctive slang associated with particular subcultures). This unusual study is a reminder that people can become outsiders for reasons other than breaking the law.

Who makes the laws?

Becker's theory is unusual in approaching deviance from two sides; most criminal sociologists focus only on deviants. Becker also examined how the laws that identify people as deviants come to be made.

Task 3.3

Recall what functionalists and Marxists say about who makes the rules and laws of society.

Guidance

Functionalists describe a consensus, whereas Marxists suggest that only one group is responsible.

Becker identified a more interactionist process behind the making and enforcing of laws than did structuralist sociologists.

Law creation

Becker's theory of law creation includes the following points:

- Moral entrepreneurs identify a situation that offends their values. These crusading reformers, typically from higher social classes, form pressure groups and make it their mission to change the law.
- A state of alertness (and often fear) is aroused in the community by the publicity of shocking cases.
- The public puts pressure on the government to investigate the matter.
- If the government takes it seriously, a commission gathers opinions from interested groups and data from experts.

- Eventually, experts may influence the exact drafting of legislation in favour of their own professions, with results that are rather different from those intended by the moral entrepreneurs.

Thus the law results from interaction between groups.

Law enforcement

Becker's theory of law enforcement includes the following points:
- Once the law is passed, the police decide how to enforce it. They may not be interested in its moral justifications, only in the need to do their job and maintain public respect.
- The police have discretion, so offenders who break minor laws but apologise may escape punishment, whereas rule-breakers who challenge the police may be arrested.
- Professional criminals may be able to 'fix' their cases and avoid punishment, whereas amateurs lack this ability.
- All police forces have priorities, so the enforcement of some laws may be neglected in favour of more pressing issues.

Therefore, whether a person who commits a deviant act is labelled as a deviant depends on the priorities of the enforcement officer and, if he/she decides to confront the law-breaker, on the nature of the interaction.

Interactionist studies of deviance

How is stuttering explained?

Edwin Lemert (1967) agreed with Becker that official responses to primary deviance often generate secondary deviance. This is the case in American penal institutions, where deviant subcultures develop, despite attempts to rehabilitate the prisoners.

Lemert also studied patterns of drinking and stuttering in various societies. For example, he observed that stuttering is a common problem in Japan, where stutterers may be rejected from better schools, from certain professions and in matchmaking. Some Japanese stutterers withdraw from society and live in isolated villages. There is so much desire to be cured that 'stuttering-correction schools' and mail-order booklets on stuttering are profitable ventures. The pressure in Japanese families to succeed academically leads to parents paying undue attention to natural verbal slips in infancy. This adds to children's anxiety when they speak, leading to the secondary deviance of frequent stuttering.

In contrast, Samoans believe that stutterers are born that way, so they make no attempt to treat the condition. Stutterers are not rejected by particular occupations and they remain socially integrated. As a result of the lack of social response, stuttering is relatively rare in Samoa.

How real is mental illness?

Some sociologists view mental illness less as a medical phenomenon than as a social construction, sharing Becker's view of the importance of definitions. Note the *synoptic link between health and deviance*.

With the exception of physical brain diseases, Thomas Szasz (1960) referred to mental illness as a myth. In most cases, people are judged to be mentally ill by comparing their ideas and modes of behaviour with those of the observer and most of society. The concept of illness 'implies deviation from a clearly defined norm'. However, the norms of mental health are far more difficult to establish than the norms of physical health. The judgements made are ethical or sometimes legal, based on what is regarded as desirable or permitted behaviour, yet the cures proposed are medical — for example, the use of tranquillisers — and are, therefore, inappropriate. Szasz argued that phenomena now regarded as mental illnesses should be regarded instead as 'expressions of man's struggle with the problem of *how* he should live…The notion of mental illness thus serves mainly to obscure the everyday fact that life for most people is a continuous struggle'. The potential for universal human happiness is a fantasy, although we can try to minimise social and economic problems. However, rather than face this, society prefers to label those who discover and react to the truth as mentally ill, just as in the past vulnerable women were scapegoated as witches.

In 1973, D. L. Rosenhan persuaded eight psychiatrically 'normal' people to present themselves at different psychiatric hospitals in the USA, claiming to hear voices in their heads. They used pseudonyms but otherwise always told staff the truth. Once admitted, they no longer claimed to hear voices and behaved normally. Despite the participants requesting to be discharged almost immediately, the staff diagnosed all but one as schizophrenic and interpreted their subsequent behaviour in terms of mental illness. For example, they described those making the notes that Rosenhan had requested as exhibiting obsessive-writing behaviour. It took an average of 19 days for them to be discharged. The 'visitors' that Rosenhan sent to check on the participants' behaviour confirmed that it was normal. Therefore, the views of the staff that the participants were mentally ill was based on expectation and context. The experiment demonstrated that the label of insanity is difficult to dispel, however ill-founded it may be. Rosenhan's published study was called 'On being sane in insane places'.

Task 3.4

Suggest reasons why the following types of people might have been regarded as mentally ill, and by whom:

- soldiers returning from the frontline during the First World War, who proclaimed that to continue fighting was immoral
- founders of new religious sects
- housewives responding to domestic drudgery by frequent crying
- people publicly opposing communism in the former USSR
- scientists claiming discoveries contrary to prevailing beliefs — for example, that the Earth goes round the sun
- homosexuals

Guidance

These cases all involve relatively powerful groups whose interests or beliefs would be undermined by the stance taken by the 'deviant'.

How might labelling reinforce mental illness?

Lemert (1967) noted that 'paranoid people are those whose inadequate social learning leads them, in situations of unusual stress, to incompetent social reactions'.

Job loss, divorce or failure to gain promotion may lead some people to react unconventionally for a while. The reaction of other people is often to avoid them or to engage in spurious (false or shallow) interaction, such as humouring or ignoring them, which adds to their sense of rejection. Thus, in response to social exclusion, idiosyncrasy (primary deviance) turns into more pronounced paranoia (secondary deviance)

In the research paper 'Institutionalism in mental hospitals' (*British Journal of Social and Clinical Psychology*, 1 February 1962), J. K. Wing studied male schizophrenic patients at two good quality hospitals. He compared the attitudes and behaviour of those who had been residents for different periods of time, controlled for other variables, such as age. He conducted interviews with patients and their nurses and analysed behaviour checklists completed by nurses. The clinical symptoms of schizophrenia did not, on average, increase markedly over time, but the signs of institutionalisation did. Patients received fewer visitors, took less interest in the outside world — including watching television — took less responsibility for themselves, increasingly wanting help with washing and dressing, and had fewer plans for the future. They became increasingly reluctant to leave hospital. Thus, the patients entered hospital with 'primary disabilities' (the chronic symptoms of schizophrenia) but over 40% gradually gained the 'secondary disabilities' of dependence and the inability to fit back into life in the outside world, even if 'cured'.

Task 3.5

Wing stated that 'the recent development of multiple admissions of short duration, with adequate support during periods out of hospital, is bound to have a beneficial effect in preventing secondary handicaps, if it is carried out efficiently'.

Investigate how community care has largely replaced psychiatric hospitals by visiting the website of Mind (The National Association for Mental Health) and skimming the history of the mental health section, particularly the key dates.

www.mind.org.uk/Information/Factsheets/History of mental health

The reality of mental illness

Wing expressed no doubts that the psychiatric patients in his study were hospitalised because of genuine symptoms. There is plenty of evidence suggesting that certain types of mental illness may have physical causes:

- Bipolar depression is linked to a defective chromosome.
- Postnatal depression and premenstrual syndrome are hormone-related.
- Schizophrenia may be attributable, in part, to excessive amounts of dopamine in the brain.
- Alzheimer's disease is linked with at least three genes and with abnormal brain deposits.
- Alcohol and other drugs can trigger mental illnesses.

In addition, some provoking agents can result in mental illnesses, such as:

- trauma (post-traumatic stress syndrome and phobias)
- long-term stress resulting from poverty, discrimination or relationship problems.

These points undermine the view that mental illness is socially constructed.

Do the media amplify deviance?

Interactionists suggest that media coverage of deviance makes acts of deviance likely to escalate, as well as increasing public fear. This is known as media amplification of deviance. In the context of crime, it can happen as a result of the following:

- copy-catting, giving people ideas for new types of crime
- attracting curious or bored people to potential trouble spots
- pressurising police to stop and search more people for offences that they might have overlooked previously
- suspects reacting angrily to the crackdown by resisting arrest or fighting with police
- bystanders sympathetically supporting suspects that the police are trying to arrest, escalating into riots
- sensitising the public to notice and report offences

Task 3.6

Which of the above bullet points result in actual increases in crime and which lead only to greater recording of pre-existing crime?

In *Folk Devils and Moral Panics* (1972), Stanley Cohen explored the nature of a moral panic, defined as follows:

> A condition, episode, person or group of persons emerges to become defined as a threat to societal values and interests; its nature is presented in a stylised and stereotypical fashion by the mass media; the moral barricades are manned by editors, bishops, politicians and other right-thinking people; socially accredited experts pronounce their diagnoses and solutions; ways of coping are evolved or (more often) resorted to; the condition then disappears, submerges or deteriorates and becomes more visible.
>
> S. Cohen, *Folk Devils and Moral Panics* (1972)

Since 1945, a recurrent type of moral panic in Britain has related to the emergence of various youth subcultures, particularly those associated with violence, such as teddy boys and skinheads. Unpopular groups frequently targeted by the media are known as folk devils. Cohen regarded his work as part of the 'sceptical revolution in criminology', following on from Becker's ideas about the 'transactional nature of deviance' — the notion that deviance is created by society. How agents of social control and the public respond to particular events depends on what information they receive. Therefore, the media can arouse concern by the 'facts' they select and by operating as 'agents of moral indignation'.

Cohen studied disturbances at English seaside resorts from 1964–66, which involved mods and rockers. Easter Sunday 1964 was wet and some of the youths taking a break in Clacton were bored and became involved in scuffles. It is true that windows were broken and beach huts damaged. However, by interviewing people present and checking their accounts for internal consistency, Cohen established that press coverage greatly exaggerated the seriousness of events.

Typical rockers were unskilled manual workers who favoured leather and motorbikes; mods tended to be semiskilled manual workers, who wore suits protected by parkas, and rode Italian scooters. However, the fights at Clacton were less between followers of these styles than between Londoners and locals, many of whom followed neither fashion.

Nevertheless, press appetite for novelty meant that mods and rockers became polarised and identified as enemies, so that fights between them became increasingly likely. More and more young people adopted these styles over subsequent months.

The media created a self-fulfilling prophecy by assuming that mods and rockers were planning revenge attacks on each other and interviewing them on television about where they next intended to strike. While descriptions of the 'riot', 'orgy of destruction' and 'battle' of Clacton alarmed some members of the public, others, particularly the young, visited seaside resorts on subsequent bank holidays to seek out excitement. Inevitably, this influx, the sense of expectancy and the drafting in of extra police led to more confrontations than usual. As the moral panic progressed, the

Mods and rockers running riot in 1964

police became sensitised by the media to view young people of certain appearances as sources of trouble. Police tactics became harsher, which led to worsening relationships with holidaymakers. There were more assaults on police, more arrests and punitive sentences, which resulted in a spiral of hostility and further media panic.

> Once an episode of collective behaviour has appeared, its duration and severity are determined by the response of the agencies of social control.
>
> S. Cohen, *Folk Devils and Moral Panics* (1972)

Cohen noted the irresponsible commercial exploitation of folk-devil images. Seaside shops whose owners complained about loss of trade because of the disturbances, advertised, for example 'the latest mod sunglasses' and other goods, exaggerating group differences.

How did the panic about mods and rockers originate? Cohen argued that older people felt uneasy about the new 'permissive society' and the growing affluence of the young, often reflected in bizarre fashions. As working hours became shorter and motorbikes and scooters were increasingly available, young people seemed to be flooding into places of leisure, seeking excitement, and this was perceived as an unwelcome change.

Is drug taking amplified by the media?

In 'The myth of the drug taker in the mass media' in S. Cohen and J. Young (eds) *The Manufacture of News* (1973), Jock Young took a similar line to Cohen. He argued that conventional values of working hard and being rewarded by pleasure are disrupted by hedonistic drug taking. The notion that marijuana gives pleasure to those who have not earned it is difficult for the public to accept, so the media provide a more palatable message.

> *Deviancy is unpleasurable*…Only the sick person, impelled by forces beyond his control, would find himself involved in such an activity.
>
> J. Young, 'The myth of the drug taker in the mass media' in
> S. Cohen and J. Young (eds) *The Manufacture of News* (1973)

Thus, marijuana users are viewed as either evil pushers or as victims who may easily become addicted to harder drugs and plummet to destruction.

> The mass media portrayal of the drug taker is not a function of random ignorance but a coherent part of a consensual mythology…Although much of its world view is fantasy, its effects are real enough. For by fanning up moral panics about drug use, it contributes enormously to public hostility to the drug taker and precludes any rational approach to the problem.
>
> J. Young, 'The myth of the drug taker in the mass media' in
> S. Cohen and J. Young (eds) *The Manufacture of News* (1973)

In another article, 'The amplification of drug use', Young summarised his participant observation study of the relationship between the police and marijuana smokers in Notting Hill between 1967 and 1969. In his view, the police were socially segregated from hippy marijuana smokers and accepted the media myths about them. Though the drug-taking activities were initially relatively harmless, in Young's view, police crackdowns in response to the moral panic led to a deviancy amplification spiral, with drug takers resorting to new types of behaviour closer to the myth. The results are indicated in the right-hand column of Table 3.2.

According to Young and Cohen, the reasons behind such moral panics, with their deviancy amplification spirals and increased human suffering, is that 'the media have learnt that the fanning up of moral indignation is a remarkable commercial success'. An opposing view is that media coverage sometimes discourages deviance by publicising the risks. This is known as the Nemesis effect, after the goddess of retribution. The public may also be warned about new crimes, reducing offenders' chances of success.

Table
3.2

Deviancy amplification

Initial reality	Media fantasy	Results of panic
Typical Bohemian scene of psychologically stable people with friendly visiting between users and non-users	Isolated unstable drug takers living in socially disorganised area	Drug takers segregated themselves from non-users to reduce likelihood of detection
Hippies have oppositional values of spontaneity, hedonism, expressivity and disdain for work	Asocial individuals preyed on by wicked pushers	Paranoia developed as hippies feared detection; they became more introspective and disturbed, so working became increasingly unlikely
Drugs used irregularly, not the central focus of people's lives	Drugs as the central group activity	Drug taking became of greater value as a symbol of group defiance against perceived persecution
Marijuana users and sellers are not fixed roles; supplies irregular, often from tourists returning from abroad, so users pass them around informally	Drug pyramid of pushers linked with the criminal underworld, preying on users	Increased vigilance made it difficult for tourists to bring in marijuana, so professionals took over; criminal underworld also involved in pushing other drugs
Marijuana users disdainful of heroin addicts, unattracted by their obsessive lives	Marijuana users expected to become heroin addicts in search for 'kicks'	Marijuana users drawn closer to heroin users as both felt persecuted; turning to heroin more likely, though still rare
Marijuana use widespread in Notting Hill, with high proportions of the young trying it at some point	Small number, but increasing too fast	Increased pressure on police forced them to penetrate undetected groups, confirming the impression of a 'crime wave'; press coverage tempted more people to experiment with the drug
Effects of marijuana mildly euphoric	Exaggerated view of peaks and troughs of misery	Desperation associated with social exclusion prompted some to take harder drugs

How useful are interactionist theories?

Becker defended the interactionist approach as follows:
- The act of labelling is not offered as the *sole* explanation for crime. It would be foolish to suggest that people commit crimes simply because of expectation.

> Nevertheless, one of the most important contributions of this approach has been to focus attention on the way labelling places the actor in circumstances which make it harder for him to continue the normal routines of life and thus provoke him to 'abnormal' actions, as when a prison record makes it harder to earn a living at a conventional occupation and so disposes the possessor to move into an illegal one.
>
> H. Becker, *Outsiders* (1963)

- Becker preferred to call the perspective 'interactionist' rather than 'labelling', because his approach includes those who are not labelled, as well as those who are, as illustrated by the four-cell formulation. This reminds us that people apprehended for acts of deviance are not identical to those committing deviant acts. Therefore, trying to analyse deviance by identifying the characteristics of 'known offenders', as criminologists often do, is doomed to failure.
- Interactionist perspectives are important in drawing attention to how one party in a relationship can be disproportionately powerful and impose rules on others, while appearing to be just. Examples of such relationships are parent and child, teacher and student and welfare worker and client.
- Conservatives criticise the interactionist perspective as subversive — 'a mischievous assault on the social order' that implies that deviant acts are not necessarily 'wrong'. Left-wingers suggest the approach is insufficiently radical because it attacks low-level functionaries such as the police, 'leaving the higher-ups responsible for the oppression unscathed'.
- Becker responded to conservative and left-wing critics, saying that they were basing moral judgements on issues that had not been scientifically examined. In contrast, interactionists take a value-free approach by questioning definitions; only after these have been penetrated is it reasonable to take a moral stance. This approach is important because definitions are a form of social control.

> Elites, ruling classes, bosses, adults, men, Caucasians — superordinate groups generally — maintain their power as much by controlling how people define the world…as by the use of more primitive forms of control. The attack on hierarchy begins with an attack on definitions, labels, and conventional conceptions of who's who and what's what.
>
> H. Becker, *Outsiders* (1963)

Summary

- Becker described deviance as a social construction. Not all deviants are detected and some people are wrongly labelled, so generalisations about the characteristics of known deviants are unhelpful.
- A number of circumstances, including powerlessness, may lead to the labelling of a person who commits an act of primary deviance. A series of events then follows that make secondary deviance and a deviant career more likely.
- The interactionist explanation of how laws are made and enforced differs from functionalist and Marxist accounts. Moral entrepreneurs often begin the process.
- Lemert found evidence that particular social responses to speech errors can lead to the secondary deviance of habitual stuttering.
- Several sociologists regard mental illness as either a social construction or a condition made worse by labelling. Other evidence indicates that some mental illnesses have physical causes.
- Studies by Cohen and Young suggest that moral panics induced by the media can amplify deviance, for example in situations such as youth disturbances and drug taking.
- Interactionist theories have been questioned by both right-wing and left-wing critics but have been strongly defended by Becker.

Task 3.7

Examine the relationship between deviance and labelling. (12 marks)

Guidance

The main problem with low-mark questions covering huge topics is selecting the essentials:

- Begin by defining labelling and citing Becker's comments on the nature of deviance.
- Use the four-cell model to explain that not all deviance is so labelled and that some of those labelled are not really deviant.
- Using key vocabulary, summarise Becker's description of the process by which primary deviation, if labelled, may lead to secondary deviation.
- Briefly, refer by name to several studies that illustrate how labelling can lead to amplified deviance.
- Conclude by balancing the strengths of the interactionist position with some shortcomings.

Useful websites

- SANE

www.sane.org.uk/public_html/About_Mental_Illness/Alcohol_Drugs.shtm
- Sociology Stuff (Focus on: Inventing criminals)

www.homestead.com/rouncefield/deviance.html
- Tamara O'Hara (Focus on: Crime)

www.quia.com/pages/sociologytamara.html

Further reading

- Becker, H. (1963) *Outsiders: Studies in the Sociology of Deviance*, Free Press.
- Cohen, S. and Young, J. (eds) (1973) *The Manufacture of News: Deviance, Social Problems and the Mass Media*, Constable.
- Cohen, S. (3rd edn 2002) *Folk Devils and Moral Panics*, Routledge.

Subcultural and recent left-wing theories

A subculture is a social, ethnic, economic or age group with a particular character of its own, which exists within a culture or society. Its way of life is distinctive and may be based on different values arising from particular circumstances. These are used to justify shared behaviour patterns.

This chapter examines explanations for the formation of youth subcultures and for apparently high levels of delinquency. The traditional Marxist approach discussed in Chapter 2 focused mainly on adult crime. Marxist subculturalists at Birmingham University have examined youth deviance and media responses. Other left-wing theories — new criminology and left realism — identified disadvantaged young people's experiences of subcultures and of marginalisation. The studies mentioned present many opportunities for making *synoptic links with work, unemployment and leisure, poverty and media* and the *themes of youth and gender* run throughout.

How do functionalists explain youth culture?

In 1956, S. N. Eisenstadt analysed the functions of youth culture in *From Generation to Generation*. In some simple societies, an initiation ceremony at puberty establishes an individual's maturity in the eyes of the community. However, youths in Britain and other advanced industrial societies exist in a state of limbo for years, not treated consistently as either adults or children. Together with the hormonal stresses of adolescence, this creates an uncertainty of identity, which is best alleviated by spending time with peers who are in the same situation. According to functionalists, peer groups have a problem-solving role, providing social support during the period of transition between childhood and adulthood.

This explanation assumes that all the young of a particular generation share similar experiences, so the broad term youth culture may be employed. In contrast, other sociologists emphasise the very different conditions in which the young of various ethnic groups, classes, sexes and localities grow up, sharing sets of values specific to their backgrounds. They indicate this by the term subculture.

When did teenagers emerge as a distinctive group?

In 1959, Mark Abrams wrote *The Teenage Consumer*. After the war, some teenagers had, for the first time, more disposable money and leisure than older people. They could afford the new products of mass culture — fashion, magazines, records, scooters and motorbikes. They spent money hedonistically before assuming adult responsibilities, using it to create a separate identity from older people. While Abrams did not interpret this as rebellion, others did.

They were alarmed by the unconventional appearance of teddy boys, a youth subculture of the early 1950s. Teds dressed in long jackets or 'drapes' of vivid colours and often with velvet collars, drainpipe trousers, socks in shocking pink or green, thick-soled 'brothel-creeper' shoes and bootlace ties. Many lived in depressed areas and had dead-end jobs. They sought release through American rock-and-roll music and by strutting about in their spectacular outfits. They were involved in gang fights, vandalism and race riots, which drew sociologists' attention to juvenile crime committed in groups, particularly by working-class males.

Teddy boys

Why is so much crime apparently committed by groups of juveniles?

According to recent official crime statistics for England and Wales, peak ages for offending are 18 to 21 years for males and 15 to 17 years for females. Interactionists suggest that these figures are amplified by police suspicion of young people. However, self-report studies generate similar patterns. Lack of parental supervision of teenagers during the period of their lives before they have major responsibilities to occupy and constrain them may be a significant factor. Peer pressure is undoubtedly another.

Task 4.1

Consider links between the reasons suggested above for teenage delinquency and Hirschi's control theory. (see Chapter 1, pp. 15–17).

Guidance
Look particularly at what Hirschi said about commitment and involvement.

How do new subcultures evolve?

Albert Cohen (1955) in *Delinquent Boys: The Culture of the Gang* suggested subcultures evolve in a series of steps. He went on to apply this idea to juvenile delinquency.

- People are sometimes unable to reach society's goals — for example, working-class boys may not succeed at school.
- The resulting status frustration is unpleasant and becomes a psychogenic (emotional) problem needing solution.
- To justify relinquishing these goals, people must change their frames of reference. They persuade themselves that the goals are not worth pursuing by adopting different values.
- However, the solution of rejecting mainstream values may create new problems of social rejection. Only a minority of people can cope as 'loners'. Others, who cannot identify like-minded people, suffer neurosis as a result.
- More often, people seek a subculture with a congenial frame of reference. These are not necessarily 'ready made' but a product of interaction.
- New subcultures evolve gradually as several people with similar problems of adjustment to the mainstream gravitate towards each other, behaving in slightly unconventional ways as exploratory gestures. The reactions of approval or disapproval by other potential group members act as cues and agreed modes of behaviour and values develop gradually in a process of mutual conversion.
- Rejecting conventional norms may invite hostility from outsiders. To protect themselves from concern about this, members of a subculture may adopt contemptuous attitudes to the wider society, particularly to its authority figures.
- Members of a subculture become increasingly dependent on the subculture for friendships and for validation of their views and status.
- Conduct that would particularly offend mainstream values may be adopted to gain inverted status within the subculture.
- Cohen explained the apparently pointless acts of destruction or daring frequently committed by American juvenile delinquents as a collective response to status

denial, gaining them subcultural prestige and affording them some revenge against the establishment that had failed to value them.

Delinquency and subcultural values

In the 1960s, American and British sociologists tried to establish whether groups of working-class youths did indeed become delinquent because of subcultural values, as Cohen had described.

Task 4.2

Consider each of the following studies and decide whether each group held values different from those of mainstream society.

American studies

R. Cloward and L. Ohlin, *Delinquency and Opportunity* (1961)

Young people unlikely to succeed in conventional ways may be drawn into the **illegitimate-opportunity structure** in their area. There may be a criminal subculture willing to teach youngsters to commit minor offences and how to sell stolen goods for them. By adulthood, offenders will have joined a network of professional criminals. Alternatively, an area may offer entry into a conflict subculture of gang warfare or a retreatist subculture of drugs or alcoholism.

This is similar to Merton's strain theory, except that the emphasis is less on individual choice than on seeking the solidarity of a subculture.

D. Matza, *Delinquency and Drift* (1966)

Young people **drift** into crime because of their lack of responsibilities. They frequently stop offending when they become family breadwinners. Everyone has **subterranean values** (the desire to follow instincts), but 'respectable' people repress these most of the time, whereas juvenile offenders do not. This explains their motivation.

Further evidence that juvenile offenders are more normal than they seem is provided by the excuses that they use when explaining their offences. They know such acts are usually wrong, but employ **techniques of neutralisation**, supplying reasons why in this particular situation the act was justified — they had to support a friend, or the victim deserved it, or it was even an act also performed by the accusers.

Walter B. Miller, *Lower Class Culture as a Generating Milieu of Gang Delinquency* (1962)

In the case of 'gang' delinquency, the cultural system which exerts the most direct influence on behaviour is that of the lower-class community itself — a long established, distinctively patterned tradition with an integrity of its own — rather than a so-called 'delinquent subculture' which has arisen through conflict with middle-class culture and is oriented to the deliberate violation of middle-class norms.

Task 4.2 (continued)

The adolescent street-corner group is an important source of identity and companionship for the young male, especially if he lives in a mother-headed family. He may be ejected from the group unless he maintains his status by behaving in accordance with the focal concerns of lower-class culture, which are:

- trouble (e.g. willingness to join in assault or theft)
- toughness (e.g. acts of daring and gang fights)
- smartness (e.g. ability to outsmart, adroitness in repartee)
- excitement (e.g. seeking thrills and risk)
- fate (e.g. going with the flow)
- autonomy (e.g. independence, rejecting authority)

Between 40% and 60% of all Americans are directly influenced by lower-class culture.

British studies

D. Downes, *The Delinquent Solution* (1966)

In *Understanding Deviance* (1995) Downes and Rock assessed Downes's earlier studies of adolescent boys as follows:

> 'Status frustration', 'alienation', and 'delinquent subculture' were concepts that did not seem to fit descriptions of boys involved intermittently in offences of the fighting/joyriding/theft/vandalism variety. Typically, they were not members of structured delinquent gangs, with a marked sense of territory, leadership, hierarchy and membership. Delinquency was a *fact* of life but not a *way* of life. Educationally, their talk of school implied dissociation from its values rather than embitterment at academic failure. Occupationally, aspirations and expectations were set realistically low, consistent with their experience of dead-end jobs. Early marriage and 'settling down' were already in view.

The youths observed by Downes spent their leisure seeking fun to relieve dull working lives. Their presence in the street, often engaging in rowdy behaviour, made them highly visible to the police.

Guidance

You may feel that Cloward and Ohlin's study is closest to Cohen's. The lower-class culture described by Miller is rather large for a subculture and the British studies fail to support the idea of a different value system. Matza's study is more controversial. Do techniques of neutralisation really suggest normal values or are they cynical attempts by people with delinquent values to talk their way out of trouble?

What was the new criminology?

None of the explanations for subcultural behaviour discussed above are Marxist, even though Downes probably empathised with frustrated working-class youths. Cohen's discussion of how new subcultures develop is predominantly interactionist, focusing on the negotiation of roles. Cohen's account of mods and rockers (pp. 44–46) and Cohen and Young's account of marijuana smokers (p. 46) are more concerned with the social construction of, and social reaction to, deviance, rather than with inequalities.

In 1973, in *The New Criminology*, Ian Taylor, Paul Walton and Jock Young proposed a broader approach. They identified the need to combine Marxist structuralism and social constructionism with smaller-scale examination of subcultural interaction, the responses of deviants to agents of social control and vice versa. This new criminology approach made connections between the following:

- **Wider origins of the deviant act** Structural analysis of the effects of rapidly changing economic and political conditions in advanced industrial societies on families, subcultures and individuals, with the focus on inequalities of wealth and power.
- **Immediate origins of the deviant act** Recognition that some people may consciously choose deviance in situations where others might not. Social psychology might provide explanations.
- **The deviant act** People may wish to behave in particular ways but be constrained by local circumstances and have to choose differently. A gang may reject a deviant who may then adopt a retreatist mode instead. Accounts of social dynamics are helpful in explaining which subcultures individuals join.
- **Immediate origins of social reaction** The public or police may ignore the deviant act or respond harshly, depending on how they exercise discretion and view the deviant. This is interactionist territory.
- **Wider origins of deviant reaction** Political theory needs to explain why some actions are punished harshly by the police and courts. As with the first bullet point, this invites Marxist explanations.
- **Effect of social reaction on the deviant's further action** Analysis of secondary deviation needs greater acknowledgement of deviants making informed choices than is implied by interactionists.
- **The nature of the deviant process as a whole** Macrosociological explanations of deviance are essential to convey the impact of enormous economic and political forces on criminal action and reaction. In addition, less deterministic interpretations of interactionist theories are required, producing a complex but thorough explanation of deviance.

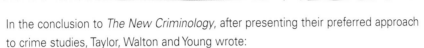

Task 4.3

In the conclusion to *The New Criminology*, after presenting their preferred approach to crime studies, Taylor, Walton and Young wrote:

> It is obvious that our endeavours need now to be supplemented with a concrete application of the formal model…to empirical cases.

Suggest a reason why the authors have not as yet carried out a study following their own guidelines.

Guidance

They described such an attempt as an 'onerous enterprise'.

What were the achievements of Marxist subculturalists?

In the 1970s, several sociologists at Birmingham University adopted a Marxist subcultural perspective not unlike the approach suggested by the new criminologists. A study by Phil Cohen in 1972 attributed the growth of East End subcultures to the loss of the traditional working-class community. After extensive bombing during the Second World War, the area was extensively rebuilt and this disrupted people's lives:

- People were rehoused in impersonal high-rise flats, which were cheaper to build than houses.
- Extended families that had lived in the same street were separated, which destroyed traditional support networks.
- Parents with young families felt isolated and relationships sometimes deteriorated.
- The nature of the community changed as successful locals moved out and speculators rented out vacated housing to immigrants.

In addition, patterns of work changed:

- Manual work in the docks declined with automation.
- Family-owned corner shops and small businesses were replaced by supermarkets offering mainly dead-end jobs.
- Traditional crafts that children had learnt from their parents were replaced by automated techniques controlled by a few specialist technicians.
- New service industries provided few opportunities for working-class males.

Cohen suggested that the new rootlessness, combined with large-scale unemployment, led groups of working-class youths to band together, asserting ownership of a 'patch' (local area) as a substitute for the lost community and to show property speculators that they were in control. Such gangs often fought to defend their territories against other youths, even though the real cause of their insecurity was capitalism. The styles of dress adopted by such groups reflected their economic situation:

- The smart suits of mods expressed their desire to be upwardly mobile, even though this was often unrealistic.
- Skinheads dressed like the traditional manual workers they wished they could be, and originally took up reggae, the protest music of poor West Indians.

Thus, Cohen identified the immediate context of subcultures and incorporated Marxist ideas about the effects of capitalist speculation on the working class.

What is the significance of youth styles?

Cohen's suggestion that the dress and music adopted by particular youth groups could be meaningfully interpreted was developed at Birmingham University's Centre for Contemporary Cultural Studies (CCCS), using semiology — the analysis of signs to understand hidden ideological meanings.

A collection of Marxist subculturalist research, *Resistance through Rituals*, edited by S. Hall and T. Jefferson in 1976, argued that youth subcultures choose styles that reflect negative attitudes to the prevailing culture and their own oppositional values. Clothing and hairstyles adopted by working-class youths are designed to shock, creating a sense of symbolic power that compensates for the wearers' lack of real power in a capitalist society. The studies explored deviance from the norm rather than crime, though some of the youth subcultures frequently engaged in delinquency.

Cultural responses of the teds

Like Phil Cohen, Tony Jefferson attributed the formation of the teddy boy subculture to the destruction of working-class communities and their aggression to their defence of territory, particularly against immigrants, whom they mistakenly believed took their jobs.

Their uniform reflected the proletarianisation of an upper-class style — the slick city gamblers of 1950's American western films, who gained 'high, albeit grudging, status for the ability to live smartly, hedonistically and by their wits in an urban setting'.

Teddy boys' outfits were invested with symbolism that reflected their aspirations, so insults relating to their appearance were met with extreme aggression.

The skinheads and the magical recovery of community

John Clarke developed Cohen's interpretation of skinhead behaviour, identifying their desire for roots (territoriality) as one reason why football hooligans aggressively defend their 'end'. Their style of dress was an attempt to 'recreate the inherited imagery of the community in a period in which the experiences of increasing oppression demanded forms of mutual organisation and defence'.

Skinheads with typically shaven heads, narrow-fitting jeans and heavy boots

Clarke used the word 'magic' to suggest that their adoption of a style worn by heavy-manual workers in the past enabled them to delude themselves that they had the steady jobs and masculine status of family breadwinners. Every item of their appearance contributed to this effect:

- masculine short hair or shaven heads reflecting the working-class need to combat head lice
- granddad shirts without collars, from the days when laundering was expensive, or tee-shirts to simulate workers' singlets
- narrow trousers or jeans — practical and hardwearing
- braces — more comfortable than belts for manual workers
- heavy boots as worn by manual workers and soldiers — useful in fights

Skinheads felt excluded from the middle-class hippy scene of the late 1960s. They chose instead to identify with the hard image of life in the East End associated with the Kray brothers. They collected on street corners, in pubs and at football matches and, to emphasise their traditionally British macho self-image, engaged in 'Paki-bashing' and attacked males wearing 'feminine' clothes.

Hippies

Stuart Hall ('The hippies: an American moment', in *Student Power*, J. Nagel (ed.) Merlin Press, 1969) examined the style adopted by American hippies and to a lesser extent by British students. Though middle class, many hippies were idealistic about left-wing movements and identified with the poor by wearing ragged old clothes. Native Americans were another exploited group, so hippies chose to wear moccasins, headbands and beads to express their solidarity. The late 1960s was a time of relative affluence for the middle classes. More young people than ever before were university students or could afford to take time out and survive on state benefits or casual work.

TopFoto

Hippies wore headbands and beads to express their solidarity with Native Americans

Their interest in meditation was reflected in eastern styles, such as batik kaftans. Floral motifs worn by both sexes symbolised 'flower power', passive resistance and the celebration of nature. Commitments to international brotherhood and hedonism in opposition to the 'rat race' of capitalism were expressed through peace logos, bells and sandals. Some hippies lived in self-sufficient communes, singing, dancing, sharing partners and taking drugs. Rejecting conformity, men had long hair and wore bright colours and jewellery. Hippies consciously invented their own styles to express a radical counterculture, a subculture that opposed mainstream values.

Revolting style

In an influential book, *Subculture, the Meaning of Style* (1979), Dick Hebdige consolidated CCCS work. He described subcultural fashions as 'intentional communication' and, with deliberate ambiguity, 'revolting style'.

Punks chose a bricolage (creative and unconventional selection) of 'objects borrowed from the most sordid of contexts' to add to their outfits, such as lavatory chains, tampons, bondage items, swastikas, bin liners and scraps of school uniform defiled with graffiti or dried blood. These signified a 'voluntary assumption of outcast status'. The style arose as the economy declined in the late 1970s and punks used it to protest against wide-scale unemployment.

Some members were working class; others were art students intrigued by the extremes of style. Hairstyles such as Mohicans in shocking colours, outlandish make-up and torn clothing fastened with giant safety pins were intended to express disdain for conventions (the opposite of interview clothes) and to emphasise the poverty of unemployed youth. Songs had a threatening tone and anti-establishment lyrics, such as 'Anarchy in the UK' by the Sex Pistols. The names of musicians, for example Sid Vicious, expressed symbolic violence.

Punks dressed to express disdain of conventions

While individual members might not have been fully conscious of the symbolism of the styles they adopted, in 'semiotic guerrilla warfare' the subculture as a whole deliberately selected explosive mixtures of items to transgress conventional boundaries. In confrontational dressing 'the rule would seem to be, if the cap doesn't fit, wear it'. Punk clothes were 'the sartorial (clothing) equivalent of swear words'; mods used scooters in large formations as a 'menacing symbol of group solidarity'.

How convincing were Marxist subcultural studies?

Hebdige admitted that some subcultural styles were difficult to 'read'. The significance of punks wearing the swastika was unclear because in general they were not racist. Perhaps it was simply intended to shock, or maybe the contradictions within the style expressed a broader message about contemporary meaninglessness.

This discussion illustrates the subjectivity of semiological interpretations compared with positivist methods. Stanley Cohen criticised the CCCS research, suggesting that Marxists interpret behaviours as class resistance, even when members of a subculture do not view their actions in this way. The Marxist defence is that adoption of particular styles may be a subconscious reaction. However, if it is a subconscious reaction, then the youths are, therefore, unable to recognise and articulate it. This can be met with the counter-argument that, if subconscious, such motives cannot be proved to exist by Marxists. This is a circular argument — one that goes nowhere.

Another question is to what degree the subcultural styles *continue* to reflect the oppositional attitudes that sociologists identify. Radical styles rapidly become commercialised for general consumption by high-street capitalists. So, respectable members of the community adopt, for example, slightly spiky hairstyles or kaftans to look 'in touch'. The very attempts by subcultures to resist capitalism result in further profit for those they oppose.

Some subculturalists have been criticised for making light of serious crime. Marsh, Rosser and Harré were not part of the CCCS group but they conducted a similar study. In *The Rules of Disorder* (1980) they suggested that what occurred at football matches was often symbolic violence. After matches, fans told exaggerated stories of how many opposition supporters they had injured, and media 'hype' reflected this. Teenaged boys, denied dignity by the rest of society, expressed their aggression to gain peer status. However, these rituals were bound by informal rules and rarely resulted in serious violence. This interpretation was rejected by Williams, Dunning and Murphy. In *Hooligans Abroad* (1984), they described the true extent of football violence and attributed it to a more complex range of causes. As will be seen below, left realists also critiqued the theory that working-class delinquency did little real harm.

Feminists have asked why subcultural theories have virtually ignored girls.

Do girls form subcultures?

In 'Girls and subcultures' (*The Subcultures Reader*, 1975), Angela McRobbie and Jenny Garber suggest that 'Girls' subcultures may have become invisible because the very term "subculture" has acquired strong masculine overtones'.

Reasons why girls rarely feature in studies such as those conducted at the CCCS include the following:
- Most researchers into subcultures have been male and have focused on male groups. Females may be unresponsive to male researchers. For example, girls simply giggled when Paul Willis, studying bikers, asked them questions.
- In the 1950s, girls' wages were not as high as those of boys, so they were less likely to adopt extremes of dress. Those interested in mod or teddy boy styles often confined themselves to less spectacular changes in make-up or hairstyle.
- Girls were more focused on marriage than their male counterparts. They were discouraged from hanging about in streets because this was taken as a sign of promiscuity and they had to be careful not to 'get into trouble'. Good reputations mattered because working-class girls would be financially dependent on their husbands.
- Preteen and teenaged girls spent leisure time in each others' houses, practising dance steps and hairstyles and adoring pop stars as a rehearsal for later

encounters with 'real' males. Privatised subcultural activities are inaccessible to researchers.

- The teenybopper culture was commercial in origin. It was a response to pop music and teen media and was possibly less interesting to researchers than the bricolage adopted by predominantly male subcultures.

Nevertheless, some became teddy girls, present at nightclubs and on the fringes of street disturbances. However, they were more often there as girlfriends, rather than in their own right. Being a rocker conflicted with conventional femininity and the few seen on motorbikes were always on the back seat.

More girls were mods because the style was neat and fairly acceptable to parents, It consisted mainly of a rather white face, cropped hair and dark eye make-up. In the mid-1960s, more single working-class girls began to live in bedsits away from home. The first Brook clinic opened in 1964, making contraception available, so girls were freer to engage in street culture, although early marriage was still a focus.

In the late 1960s and early 1970s, increased access to university gave many middle-class girls several years of unsupervised freedom. Therefore, the hippy subculture attracted higher proportions of females than earlier subcultures. The movement was 'an empowering space for women', enabling some to experiment sexually, engage in social protest and explore feminism. More recently, girls have been significantly involved in subcultures such as punk, Gothic and grunge.

Are there oppositional youth subcultures now?

Since the 1990s, sociologists have observed that the age of spectacular youth subcultures is over. Postmodernists such as Jean Baudrillard argue that social class is no longer an important source of identity, and, instead of creating radical styles, young people simply buy fashions they like in shopping malls. Steve Redhead attributed rave subculture to young people's desire for fun, denying any symbolic meaning. Choices of fashion do not correlate with patterns of social stratification or sets of values, so groups who adopt a particular type of outfit are termed style tribes, rather than subcultures.

While postmodernists focus on consumption patterns, other sociologists insist that social inequalities still generate subcultures. In several studies since the late 1980s, Mairtin Mac an Ghaill and Tony Sewell have identified Asian and African-Caribbean anti-school subcultures that result in conflict with teachers, underachievement, expulsion and subsequent employment problems. Echoing the semiological approach adopted by the CCCS, Sewell, in discussing a school's attempts to influence pupils' haircuts, wrote: 'All black people's hairstyles are political: they are invested with social and symbolic meaning'.

How did the CCCS Marxists explain moral panics?

The interactionists Stanley Cohen and Jock Young suggested that moral panics arise from media desire to increase readership. Marxists, however, identified political motives. Stuart Hall and CCCS colleagues drew attention to public fears over mugging in *Policing the Crisis: Mugging, the State, and Law and Order* in 1978. Hall identified a point when the British government was particularly unpopular and had been challenged by student protests, strikes, demonstrations and bloodshed in Northern Ireland. 1972 was 'a year of sustained and open class conflict', a crisis of hegemony when widespread unrest threatened, unless the public could be united against a common enemy and persuaded to accept an increased police presence.

According to Hall, street robberies were not dramatically increasing, but in 1972, the media directed public attention to muggings, particularly by young black men. Longstanding worries about uncontrolled youth and immigrants undermining 'the British way of life' were whipped up in order to divert attention from government failures. American media in the 1960s had been preoccupied with family 'disorganisation' among ghetto blacks, high rates of violent robberies and racial tensions, and the UK press in 1972 predicted that the same would happen in Britain.

When three Handsworth youths of mixed ethnicity robbed an Irish labourer of cigarettes and 30 pence, editorials demanded harsh sentences to stem the tide of evil. The judge sentenced the 16-year-old 'ringleader' — despite his broken-home background and guilty plea — to 20 years imprisonment. Some newspapers commented that the father he had never known was West Indian and 'pursued the race theme'. Marxists claim that capitalists encourage racism to divide and rule the working class; such coverage lends support to this theory.

In this situation of heightened fear, harsher policing was publicly welcomed, making riots about other issues unlikely. Ironically, police overreaction then led to amplification of crime. When they responded to the stabbing of a white youth in a scuffle at a firework display, they felt outnumbered by a 'hostile' black crowd and ended up fighting with onlookers, who were subsequently arrested. Thus police expectation of trouble from particular sections of the community can become a self-fulfilling prophecy.

How convincing is Hall's view of the mugging panic?

Hall's Marxist argument is powerful, but like other Marxists he tries to 'have it both ways'.

Task 4.4

Identify the contradiction in Hall's position:

- His main thesis is that the extent of mugging was exaggerated — capitalist media focused on street crime by an out-group in order to distract the public from government inadequacies.
- In his final chapter, Hall laments declining job prospects for black people, observing, 'acts of stealing, pick-pocketing, snatching and robbing with violence, by a desperate section of black unemployed youth, can give a muffled and displaced expression to the experience of permanent exclusion'.

Marxists claim that the media exaggerate working-class crime, yet also condemn inequalities in society that are likely to lead poorer people into street crime. It is almost contradictory to state that there is not much working-class crime and at the same time to provide reasons why it occurs. *Policing the Crisis* is no exception.

Applying the Ockham's razor principle, that the simplest explanation is often the best, it might be argued that the reasons given by Hall for the mugging moral panic are more complex than the view that 'crime waves' are sensationalised to sell newspapers.

What is New Left realism?

Sociologists sometimes modify their theories as they witness changes in society. Young's study of drug takers was primarily interactionist. Then, in *The New Criminology*, he incorporated elements of Marxism. By the time he wrote *What is to be done about Law and Order?* with John Lea in 1984, he had become a Left realist.

A **Left realist** is:

- socialist rather than Marxist. The belief is that deprivation underlies much crime and that efforts must be made to improve working-class conditions.
- realistic about the suffering of crime victims, who are often working class. Offenders have free choice and are responsible for their actions. The extent of crime, revealed particularly by local victim studies such as the Islington and Merseyside surveys, must be recognised and humane efforts made to reduce it.

Young discarded Left idealist (Marxist) explanations of crime, rejecting 'the belief that property offences are directed solely against the bourgeoisie and that violence against the person is carried out by amateur 'Robin Hoods' in the course of their righteous attempt to redistribute wealth'.

At the same time, he was wary of the New Right 'law-and-order lobby', with its determination to minimise crime without addressing social conditions.

Lea and Young revised the book in 1993, convinced that crime was increasing dramatically, with an urgent need to address it.

What are the causes of crime?

Relative deprivation

- The media present attractive images of consumer goods and myths about equality of opportunity, so that many people, although not in absolute poverty, feel frustrated that they are excluded from 'the glittering prizes of capitalist society'. This affects all classes and explains working-class, white-collar and corporate crime as most people strive for more.
- Traditional community life somewhat insulated the working class from experiencing relative deprivation; poor people often accepted the local standard of living as the norm and supported each other. However, the postwar fragmentation of working-class communities has deprived people of mutual support and made them more aware of the affluence of others.
- The number of traditional, unskilled manual and manufacturing jobs has decreased, resulting in widespread unemployment. Recently, the number of people living on below half the average income has more than doubled and, when people expect a certain standard of living, this is a crimogenic (crime-inducing) situation.

Ethnic minorities suffer the additional problem of employment discrimination. The relatively high figures for black street crime may be attributable both to relative deprivation and to discriminatory police practices.

Subculture

As Cloward and Ohlin described, in some areas, criminal subcultures provide illegitimate opportunities.

Marginalisation

Working-class people lack the influence to improve their conditions:

- The permanently unemployed have not experienced trade union activism.

- New Labour politics has no left-wing appeal, so people feel unable to influence their situation, other than by rioting.

Victims and communities

Social changes have increased the proportion of potential crime victims:

- Increased car ownership means people go out more. Their homes are left unguarded and they are more vulnerable to crimes in public places.
- Attacks on 'outsiders' are more common in culturally diverse communities; people less closely bonded may be unlikely to intervene to prevent a neighbourhood crime incident.
- Structural unemployment has reduced family stability. Parents with jobs may have to work long hours, spending less time at home supervising the young. This is not a sign of moral laxity, as the New Right suggests, but a problem of capitalism.

The criminal justice system

The police clear-up rate for many crimes is now so low (e.g. 8% for burglary) that it offers little deterrent to committed offenders. In such cases, police sometimes resort to military style/conflict policing, making maximum use of cars, surveillance and heavy-handed stop-and-searches of stereotypically suspect groups.

This contrasts with consensus/community policing in which local police, often on foot, become approachable figures in the community, visiting schools and organising leisure events for young people. Conflict policing antagonises communities; those who feel they have been treated unfairly lose respect for the law. In Los Angeles in 1992, after white police were captured on video beating a black motorist, Rodney King, a riot erupted in which 58 people were killed.

What are the solutions?

Consensus policing should replace conflict policing

Inner cities and council-housing estates are likely to experience conflict policing, worsening public relations. If the police were more accountable to elected local bodies, this would enable groups such as ethnic minorities, gays and women to discuss with them the crime problems they face and, therefore, influence police policy. Approachability would encourage ordinary people to inform them about suspected crimes. Clear-up rates would improve, which would reinforce the public perception that the police are genuinely engaged in protecting their communities against specific criminals, rather than indiscriminately targeting the young, working classes and ethnic minorities.

Regeneration of inner-city areas

More government effort is needed to encourage new enterprise in inner-city areas and in industrial towns deserted by manufacturing industries, and to retrain potential workers. This should slow the growth of an alienated underclass.

Sound welfare provision

Communities can only be expected to exercise social control and meet the police for constructive dialogue if their basic needs are met. Schools must teach democratic participation; jobs with prospects and fair wages should be created and housing conditions and welfare provision must be adequate.

Victims

Victim-support groups are needed to present recurrent problems to the rest of the community. Victim compensation and victim–offender mediation schemes are also needed.

Offenders

Instead of becoming marginalised further, ex-offenders should be assigned useful community roles, such as discussing the impacts of their crimes with youth groups. Alternatives to prison, for example community service, should be expanded, except for dangerous criminals. John Braithwaite advocates reintegrative shaming — encouraging offenders to recognise and compensate for their deeds in exchange for being accepted back into the community. Such approaches contrast strongly with the punitive measures recommended by the New Right, but are only likely to be acceptable to a 'strong, secure and democratically organised community'.

Summary

- Functionalists explained youth subcultures as responses to problems of transition from childhood to adulthood.
- The distinctive 'teenager' emerged as a result of postwar leisure and consumerism.
- Delinquent subcultures may arise as young people, who are unable to gain status at school or work, seek peer group solidarity and excitement.
- New criminologists combined small-scale examination of such behaviour with structural explanations.

- Marxist subculturalists at the CCCS focused on youth styles as expressions of oppositional values. There were few studies of girls.
- The moral panic concerning mugging in 1972 was interpreted as a response to a crisis within capitalism.
- New Left realists rejected the idealism of Marxists. They showed the extent of working-class victimisation by street criminals and advocated improvements to policing and social measures to reduce deprivation.

Task 4.5

Assess the usefulness of Marxist approaches in the understanding of crime and deviance. (40 marks).

Guidance

Draw on traditional Marxist approaches from Chapter 2 and Marxist subcultural studies and the views of new criminologists from this chapter.

Demonstrate evaluation by explaining left-realist criticisms of left idealists:

- Marxists ignore the reality of street crime, overemphasising media hype and selective policing, while victim surveys reveal that such crime is even more widespread than official statistics suggest.
- Marxists suggest street crime is redistributive; left realists reveal victims are frequently poor.
- Marxists' only solution is revolution. Left realists suggest practical measures, such as changes in policing and work-creation programmes.
- A counter-argument is that the left-realist focus on working-class and black crime shifts the balance too far away from the harm done by corporate criminals, often on a global scale, which only Marxists have adequately discussed.

After briefly comparing the various Marxist approaches with other perspectives, such as functionalism, ensure that you bring your conclusion firmly back to the strengths and weaknesses of Marxism.

Research suggestion

Choose a current youth style such as 'hoodie' wearing or a named subculture such as 'chavs'. Conduct an internet search for images and comments. Attempt a semiological reading, suggesting social reasons for the style. Compare notes with fellow students to assess the method's reliability.

Useful websites

- Sociology Central (select online resources — focus on: Culture and identity and then Subcultures)

  www.sociology.org.uk/pathway2.htm
- Risk of crime and fear of crime

  www.malcolmread.co.uk/JockYoung/RISK.htm

Further reading

- Gelder, K. and Thornton, S. (eds) (1997) *The Subcultures Reader*, Routledge.
- Hall, S. and Jefferson, T. (eds) (1975) *Resistance through Rituals: Youth Subcultures in Postwar Britain*, Hutchinson.
- Taylor, I., Walton, P. and Young, J. (1973) *The New Criminology*, Routledge.

Issues of ethnicity and global crime

Earlier chapters have examined how patterns and types of crime vary with age and social class. Attention now turns to different ethnic groups as perpetrators and victims of crime, a topic often complicated by global inequalities where crimes such as drug smuggling and terrorism are concerned. We begin by considering offences in the UK and then widen the focus to international crimes, some by TNCs and states, and examine how global organisations attempt to combat them.

What is meant by ethnicity?

Sociologists prefer the word 'ethnicity' to 'race'. Genetic research shows the impossibility of categorising people precisely according to physical features, such as skin colour and hair type. In any case, sociologists are more interested in the distinctive life styles and experiences of different groups. Ethnicity refers to identification with a specific culture, including religious practices and beliefs, languages spoken, dress and other customs. Many people, for example British Hindus, may retain cultural and family links with their country of origin and continue to identify with it, but may also accommodate many aspects of British life. Their experiences will differ from those of British Asians following other religions and from Hindus in India. Therefore, statistics and generalisations about groups such as 'Asians' need careful scrutiny.

In *Islam, Crime and Criminal Justice* (2002), Basia Spalek advocates a criminology focusing more on religious groups. For example, underrepresentation of 'Asians' in prisons obscures the overrepresentation of Muslims relative to Sikhs and Hindus; this suggests factors in need of investigation.

Often, references to 'Pakistanis' should really read 'British citizens of Pakistani ancestry' but this is simply too cumbersome. Likewise, the word 'black' may be used by sociologists for many different groups, occasionally even 'Asians'. In this chapter, its use will be confined to people of African and African-Caribbean descent.

Chapter 5

What issues of ethnicity and crime are of current concern?

Task 5.1

Consider the following news items to see whether ethnicity and crime issues have changed since Hall's (1978) study of mugging (see Chapter 4, p. 64):

- **1993** The racist murder of Stephen Lawrence, a student born in Britain of Jamaican parents, was dealt with inadequately by police. The attackers remain unpunished.
- **1995** Public disturbances occurred in a mainly Muslim area of Bradford, after police tried to stop street football. Over 300 Pakistani Muslim youths attacked a police station, petrol-bombed cars, looted non-Muslim businesses and issued death threats.
- **1998** Police established Operation Trident, an intelligence initiative against violent drugs-related crime in London's black community.
- **1999** The Macpherson Report into the Lawrence case found that 'institutionally racist' police had been negligent. The black community was 'over-policed…and underprotected'. Proposals included taking seriously any case deemed as racist by the victim, better anti-racist police training and policies to reduce institutional racism in the judicial system, schools, the NHS and other government organisations.
- **2000** The killing of 10-year-old Nigerian Damilola Taylor claimed full police attention. After several trials, black teenagers Ricky and Danny Preddie, members of the 'Young Peckham Boys' gang were found guilty of manslaughter, probably with intent to rob.
- **2001** There were riots in some northern cities. In Bradford, 500 Muslim youths took to the streets expecting a National Front rally, even though it had been banned. The rioters had prepared to combat the rally by assembling weapons and petrol bombs and enlisting outside support. They attacked police, their horses, businesses run by whites and Hindus, and set public buildings on fire. White youths retaliated, causing further damage. The Cantle Report blamed segregated communities and right-wing agitators.
- **2001** Nineteen men connected with Al-Qaeda hijacked airliners, crashing two into the World Trade Center and one into the Pentagon. Over 3000 people were killed or listed as missing. Repercussions included increased **Islamophobia**, with attacks on Muslims or suspected Muslims in the USA and Britain, and war with Afghanistan. The subsequent war in Iraq was connected indirectly.
- **2002** A Home Office study found that black youths, often in gangs, were behind the 'overwhelming majority' of mobile phone thefts and robberies in inner cities. White youths were the main victims, followed by Asians.

Task 5.1 (continued)

- **2003** Jamaican-born 7-year-old Toni-Ann Byfield was shot dead in London with her supposed father, a convicted Jamaican crack-cocaine dealer. The incident led to media discussion of a violent black culture imported by Jamaican drug dealers and the effects on the black community of poverty, single parenthood and educational failure.
- **2005** The London tube and bus bombings by four British Muslims were followed by religiously motivated attacks on Muslims and supposed Muslims throughout Britain. The anti-terror laws were extended; suspects can now be held without charge for 28 days.
- **2005** Black student Anthony Walker was killed in Merseyside in a racist murder. The young white perpetrators were swiftly found guilty.
- **2006** The shooting of an innocent Asian terror suspect by police in Forest Gate worsened community relations.
- **2006** Black teenagers Donnel Carty and Delano Brown received life sentences for fatally stabbing white lawyer Thomas ap Rhys Pryce during a mugging in London.

The items in Task 5.1 show that, while black street crime remains a problem and increasingly involves drugs and firearms, black people have also been the victims of high-profile racist murders. Since the Stephen Lawrence case, such crimes have been taken far more seriously by the criminal justice system.

Asian crime received little attention in the 1970s. Recent rioting and terrorism have, however, generated new folk devils. Reporting of such events has amplified crime, with Muslims in particular being subjected to random attacks.

Stephen Lawrence was the victim of a racist murder

What are the patterns of crime by ethnic group?

The table in Task 5.2 suggests a high level of imprisonment of black people for all the listed offences, considering that they only constitute 2% of the population. The level for Asians is fairly high for some offences only.

Sociologists have debated whether the high level of imprisonment of black people is because of racism and selective practices within the criminal justice system or because black people in the UK are disproportionately criminal.

Task 5.2

Official statistics often merge groups together, as in the table below. Study the figures and use the bottom row to compare the numbers from each ethnic group imprisoned for each type of offence with their proportion in the population.

Table 5.1 Prison population by ethnic group and self-identified ethnicity, June 2005

Offence	White	Mixed	Black or black British	Asian or Asian British	Chinese and other
Violence against person	11 974	410	1 689	829	132
Sexual offences	5 145	96	555	306	49
Robbery	6 025	348	1 500	399	44
Burglary	7 163	164	532	140	26
Theft and handling	3 459	93	313	164	29
Fraud and forgery	787	37	302	263	57
Drugs offences	6 484	381	2 861	739	150
Motoring offences	1 803	54	160	124	7
Proportion of UK population	92%	1.2%	2%	4%	0.4%

Adapted from Home Office report, *Statistics on Race and the Criminal Justice System, 2005* and National Statistics Online

Do police and the courts discriminate against ethnic minorities?

In 1966, Skolnick observed that police 'canteen culture' perpetuates stereotypes of young black males as typical offenders. However, since the Macpherson Report, the police have tried to avoid 'institutional racism'.

Ethnic minorities had long complained about being 'stopped' without foundation. Macpherson decided that all stop-and-searches should be recorded by the police together with the suspect's self-defined ethnic group. Police need reasonable grounds to suspect people before stopping them. However, under section 44 of the Terrorism Act (2000), searches can be carried out in areas designated as being at risk of terrorist attack, for example the London Underground, without grounds to suspect that the person is carrying a dangerous article.

Since 7 July 2005, the number of stop-and-searches has soared. Although police deny targeting ethnic minorities, street stops of African-Caribbean and Asian people between July and September 2005 increased twelve-fold over the same period in 2004 (IHF Report, 2006), compared with a five-fold increase in street stops of whites.

Jamine Wiedel Photolibrary/Alamy

Police stop and search an ethnic-minority suspect

Police patrol heavily inner-city and working-class areas where high proportions of ethnic minorities live. Though corporate and white-collar criminals are more likely to be white, police concentrate on street crime, which is associated more with black offenders. Zero tolerance policies in response to Blair's 'tough-on-crime' pledge are more likely to result in selective policing that targets powerless groups.

Blom-Cooper and Drabble (1982) found that, when similar acts were committed, black people were likely to be charged with more serious forms of the offence than whites. Landau and Nathan (1983) found that whites received cautions rather than being prosecuted more often than black offenders who committed similar acts.

Black offenders are more likely to plead not guilty than whites, whether through innocence or because they have more faith in trial by jury in a Crown court than they have in the judgement of a magistrate. (People pleading guilty usually receive more lenient sentences.)

Hood (1992) revealed that black people were more likely than whites to receive custodial sentences for offences that have fines or community-based punishments as alternatives. This is partly because fixed abode and stable family circumstances are taken into account. A prison record, compounded with job discrimination, makes a new career, free from crime, difficult to achieve.

Once in prison, black people are stereotyped as dangerous and are treated more harshly by officers, who overlook brutality by other inmates. Black prisoners are less likely than whites to get early release (Bowling and Phillips 2002).

Why might black Britons commit crime disproportionately?

- Left realists believe that there is a disproportionate amount of black street crime because of relative poverty, marginalisation and subculture.
- The unemployment rate for African-Caribbean men is about three times greater than that for whites; the female rate is double. This provides motivation for property crimes.
- Caribbean education encouraged children to identify with British culture, so African-Caribbeans who encounter discrimination may become disillusioned. Other minorities, such as the Chinese, have less desire to assimilate.
- In *No Future* (1984), Cashmore noted that black people came to Britain for better opportunities. According to Merton's strain theory, failure to reach goals legally often leads to innovation.
- Burney (1990) described how joining a 'posse' engaged in street robberies makes a certain style of dress and leisure affordable and provides black youngsters with group identity and confidence. Peer pressure and the desire to emulate tough older brothers combine with the view that, as police see them as criminal anyway, they might as well commit crime — a self-fulfilling prophecy.
- The black British population, like the Asian equivalent, is disproportionately young, i.e. with a greater percentage of peak-offending age.
- Recent evidence from Gilbourne, Mac an Ghaill and Sewell suggests that well intentioned teachers still have negative expectations of black students.

This may lead to classroom conflict, underachievement and exclusion from school. The exclusion rate for black students is six times higher than that for whites. Inadequate educational provision for expelled students leaves them wandering the streets with little chance of obtaining qualifications, increasing the likelihood of criminal careers. Note the *synoptic link with education*.

- Compared with Asian or white families, a higher proportion of African-Caribbean families are headed by single mothers. This may create problems in controlling the behaviour of teenaged boys who, lacking the role model of a responsible father, may copy ultra-macho older boys. This point makes a *synoptic link between crime and the family*.
- According to CCCS Marxists, in *The Empire Strikes Back* (1983), black British crime is an act of political resistance. In the past, Africans were sold into slavery and whites exploited their countries. More recently, black immigrants have experienced oppression in Britain. Crime is a means of expressing opposition to white domination. A counter-argument is that after the Second World War, first-generation black immigrants to Britain suffered overt discrimination, yet were relatively law-abiding. The second and third generations have been more involved in crime, despite being protected by anti-racist legislation and being generally more accepted.
- Rastafarian rituals involving marijuana are responsible for some African-Caribbeans breaking British laws. However, British crime surveys suggest that among 16–29-year-olds, a higher proportion of whites than blacks try drugs.
- London gun culture, gang shootings and drug trafficking have been attributed to the influence of yardies, gangsters from the impoverished backyards of Kingston, Jamaica. Recently, their traits have been mimicked by British youths attracted by their conspicuous wealth and gun-toting image.
- Some blame rap music that expresses violence, homophobia, sexism and materialism for increased gun-related violence in black communities. However, critics argue that white youths listen to rap without this effect.

To summarise the debate, it is difficult to establish the degree to which higher crime rates for some ethnic minorities reflect discrimination by the criminal justice system, in which relatively few black and Asian people are employed. On one hand, many ethnic minorities are structurally disadvantaged and so have greater motivation to commit property crimes. On the other hand, white victims are more inclined to report trivial offences when committed by non-whites. Self-report studies for 14–25-year-olds show slightly higher proportions of whites than blacks confessing to crimes (39% and 38%), with much lower figures for Indians (25%), Pakistanis (24%) and Bangladeshis (12%) (Graham and Bowling 1995).

Are ethnic minorities at greater risk of victimisation?

British Crime Survey data suggest that African-Caribbeans and south Asians are at greater risk of victimisation than whites. African-Caribbeans are disproportionately victims of burglary, robbery, theft and assault; for south Asians, the most marked differences are for vandalism, threats, robbery and theft from the person. Since the recent upsurge of Islamophobia, attacks, threats and harassment have escalated.

David Smith (1997) suggested reasons for disproportionate victimisation of ethnic minorities:

- They tend to live in more dangerous areas, with high levels of incivilities.
- There are higher proportions of young males (the population segment most often attacked).
- 'Black-on-black' crime accounts for much of the victimisation. Crime is often conducted against people of the same ethnic group, such as acquaintances or locals. Where the offending rate is high, victimisation rates often follow suit — for example, from revenge attacks.
- Racially motivated crime is common. In 2001, the Crime and Disorder Act was extended to cover 'racially and religiously aggravated offences'. If victims experience hostility based on their presumed membership of a racial or religious group, the offence is deemed more serious.

Unfortunately, the latest Home Office Report (2005) found that most racial incidents were not reported to the police, and of those that were reported, the clear-up rate was only 33%. Incidents of low-level harassment, such as throwing eggs at houses, reduce the quality of life of the victims but rarely appear in official statistics.

What research has been carried out on 'Asian' crime?

In an article in Spalek's *Islam, Crime and Criminal Justice* (2002), Marie Macey regretted the lack of published research about Asian crime, some of it having been discouraged for fear of stirring up racial hatred, particularly since 11 September 2001. Analysis is essential to inform social policies. Ignoring Asian crime or explaining it only as a response to white racism is misguided and inflames hostility among white victims and witnesses.

Macey's views about the need for open debate were echoed in August 2006, when Ruth Kelly, the Communities Secretary, launched the government's new Commission for Integration and Cohesion. She described the need to engage with the argument advanced by Trevor Phillips, chairman of the Commission for Racial Equality, that support for multiculturalism should give way to efforts to create a more integrated society.

Besides the 'conspiracy of silence', another problem is the lack of appropriate researchers. Non-Muslim sociologists may lack insider knowledge and empathy, yet there is a shortage of Asian researchers, particularly Muslims, ironically for the same reasons of educational disadvantage that may give rise to Muslim crime.

Crime in Bradford

Macey suggested reasons for a relatively high rate of street crime among young Muslim males. She used Bradford as a case study, analysing the disturbances of 1995 and 2001. Her discussion focused mainly on Pakistani Muslims, as the largest ethnic minority group, while noting that Muslims in Bradford also originate from Bangladesh and India and include well-educated Asians from eastern Africa.

Bradford riots, 2001

Demographic

Approximately 70% of British Muslims are under the age of 25, so a relatively high proportion belong to the peak age group for male offending, i.e. 14–23 years.

Social and cultural aspects

- Pakistani and Bangladeshi communities (largely Muslim) suffer higher unemployment than the Indian equivalents and have poorer educational performance. In Bradford, around half of these households have no full-time workers. Unemployed youths congregate on the streets, forming troublesome macho subcultures.
- Islamophobia compounds the racial discrimination experienced by Muslims seeking work. Islamophobia was defined by the 1997 Runnymede Report as 'unfounded hostility towards Islam, and therefore dislike or fear of all or most Muslims'.
- Chain migration from Pakistan to Britain has resulted in high Muslim concentrations in ten UK areas, including Bradford. The tendency for British Muslim men to prefer brides from Pakistan, often speaking little English, has caused the community to retain a traditional south Asian identity instead of adopting westernised attitudes.
- Family income remains low because Pakistani women who have recently arrived fail to find lucrative work and may be discouraged from doing so for cultural reasons.
- Mothers who have limited English may be unaware of their sons' criminal activities.

These points provide useful *synoptic links with the family*.

Religious aspects

- Muslim objections to usury (money lending for interest) mean that many choose houses that they can buy without mortgages. This results in overcrowded households in depressed areas, which is a crimogenic condition. Discrimination by building societies and housing authorities may also contribute.
- Some young Muslims misinterpret the *Qur'an* to justify crimes against women.

> Under the concept of izzat (honour), central to Islamic culture, women carry the entire burden of upholding family and community honour…The result is that in defence of honour, men go to inordinate lengths to monitor the appearance and behaviour of women (referred to as 'guarding' (Afshar 1994) and 'policing' (Brown 1998)…control that involves them in a spectrum of behaviour from relatively minor nuisance to murder. One example is the persistent (anonymous) telephoning of 'liberal' parents to tell them that their daughters bring disgrace to the community.

A common threat in such cases is to 'run families out of Bradford', a threat that Muslim women say is a real one.

M. Macey, 'Interpreting Islam: young Muslim men's involvement in criminal activity in Bradford', in B. Spalek (ed.) *Islam, Crime and Criminal Justice* (2002)

- Selective cultural interpretations of the *Qur'an* have resulted in attacks on prostitutes and gays. The doctrine that the world is divided into good and evil, respectively the Domain of Islam and the Domain of War, i.e. the non-Muslim world, has led some Muslims to adopt negative attitudes to westerners and members of other faiths, sometimes resulting in conflict.
- The religious requirements of long hours of mosque attendance and the learning of Arabic may adversely affect school performance. Lack of English at home and extended school absences to visit Pakistan have also been suggested as contributing to educational underachievement.

These points provide useful *synoptic links with education and religion.*

Policing practices

The 1995 Bradford disturbances were sparked off by police mishandling of unruly street behaviour. Critics suggested that they were not policing by consent, which reflects left-realist views.

A counter-argument is that police were branded as racist by criminals so that they would be reluctant to intervene in future, allowing drug dealing, pimping and the oppression of women to continue unchecked. The Ousley Report (2001) described Bradford Muslim youths as feeling immune from the law, boasting that 'the police daren't touch them for fear they'll riot'.

Separatist provocation

The British National Party has developed a specifically anti-Islamic focus and has gained votes in northern towns in which the 2001 riots occurred. However, its ability to create a climate of antagonism is more significant than its electoral potential. Muslim anticipation of BNP activity sparked off the 2001 riots, in which even children were involved in making petrol bombs. Militant Muslim groups have tried to gain young supporters in such an atmosphere, circulating inflammatory literature against both westerners and non-Islamic faiths. Both white and Muslim separatists are responsible for the continuing tension.

Territoriality

Many of the Muslim residents of Bradford interviewed by Macey deplored the riots. Some blamed them on 'plain law breaking by idiots', others on the desire of gangs to control their own territories and 'keep the police off "their" turf'.

Task 5.3

(a) Consider the crimes in Bradford that are described on page 81 from subcultural perspectives, such as those of Miller and Matza.

(b) Now apply Phil Cohen's territoriality theory.

(c) Finally, apply explanations from left realism.

Guidance

(a) To what extent were Pakistani males influenced by macho values? Did they use 'techniques of neutralisation'?

(b) Could Pakistani Muslims be described as rootless (feeling they belong nowhere), or are problems mainly structural?

(c) To what extent could the offences described be attributable to relative deprivation, marginalisation and subculture?

Why have some British-born Muslims supported terrorism?

The reasons for the terrorist acts of extremist organisations such as Al-Qaeda are too complex for discussion here, although exploring them in other sources would provide interesting *synoptic links with politics, religion and world sociology.*

TopFoto

The remains of the double-decker bus destroyed in the London bombings, 2005

Of current concern is why a few British-born Muslims were prepared to murder fellow citizens (including six Muslims) in the London bombings of 2005 and allegedly attempted to blow up transatlantic flights in 2006. These events are too recent for detailed research to have been completed. However, a number of theories have been suggested:

- Muslims have been alienated by British foreign policy, particularly since the war in Iraq. The government denies a connection between this and Islamic militancy. However, imams at universities have described the frustration of youths as their views on Iraq, the Israeli–Palestinian question and the Lebanon conflict have been ignored. Faith in western democracy has been lost.

- Muslims feel threatened by the police, particularly since the shooting of innocent men at Stockwell and Forest Gate. Stop-and-searches of people of Asian appearance have increased greatly and suspects can now be held for 28 days without charge. Since Forest Gate, some Asians have distrusted British reporting and turned to the Islamic media.
- Britain has failed to integrate its 1.5 million Muslims, of whom around 750 000 are of Pakistani origin. They have been allowed to live in 'ghettoes' and attend single-faith schools. Well-intentioned multiculturalism has created a divided society.
- In contrast, others suggest that British lack of tolerance for alternative views is to blame for Islamophobia and orientalism (Edward Said's term for Westerners' supposed tendency to view people from the East as inferior and 'other'). The resulting rejection forces minorities into oppositional groupings.
- Ahmed Versi, editor of *Muslim News*, counter-argues: 'Except in a few cases, Muslims are very well integrated in British society. The idea of non-integration is part of a stereotype that portrays Muslims as outside mainstream society.' Claims that Muslims put their religion before their nationality are based on surveys asking people to make a false choice, because most people see no conflict between the two.
- Jason Burke of the *Observer* suggests that, 'the uncertainty brought by the loss of the hierarchies and values of traditional societies' has caused moral confusion and militancy in some Muslim Pakistani immigrants.
- Ian Reader of Lancaster University suggests that Islamic networks in the UK behave like cults. They distance their members from normal social contacts and create closed societies that generate intense fanaticism and dedication. Disillusioned young men are drawn to non-violent religious groups and then progress to more extreme mosques, study groups, militant politicised training abroad and, finally, into terrorist cells.

Task 5.4

Consider how the process described by Reader is similar to the formation of an oppositional subculture described by Albert Cohen (see Chapter 4, pp. 53–54).

Guidance

Examine each step suggested by Cohen, from status frustration through the later stages of rejecting mainstream values and hostility to outsiders.

- Fred Halliday of the London School of Economics claims that internet propaganda and recruitment videos can radicalise young people from ordinary backgrounds. Those arrested after the failed London bombings of

21 July 2005 admitted to watching videos of civilian deaths in Iraq. However, according to the use-and-gratification model of media effects, people are only influenced by content that they are predisposed to accept.
- There are different styles of Islam practised in the UK. Early southern Asian immigrants followed a tolerant non-political style. However, strands associated with the Taliban, Saudi Arabian conservatism and the creation of modern Muslim states have become more influential in seminaries, radical-ising the teaching at some British mosques.

Task 5.5

Psychiatrist Mark Sagemen comments: 'Foreign policy did not create Al-Qaeda but has expanded the pool of people who want to do things. Local grievances acquire a global element and people are more willing to sacrifice themselves for a global vision.' (quoted by Jason Burke, *Observer*, 20 August 2006)

Discuss how this comment might explain how young men from places such as Bradford might become involved in terrorism.

Guidance

Focus on the 'local grievances' described in Macey's account on pages 79–81.

Crime as a global issue

Milan Rai (2006), while deploring the deprivation and discrimination experi-enced by British Muslims, identifies the main cause of the 7 July attacks as Britain's involvement in Iraq and Afghanistan, a view that is shared by many, including BBC correspondent Frank Gardner. Events such as these and the links made above between black British youths and Jamaican yardies show that, in the postmodern world, crime is often an international issue.

Some types of crime stem from global injustices and inequalities. In developing countries, people struggle to survive because:
- the crops they grow are traded unfairly
- their governments cannot provide welfare benefits because of multiple problems, including international debt

In such circumstances, it is more profitable to grow coca or opium poppies than legal crops, and citizens of affluent countries are willing to pay high prices for such goods. While drug smuggling is not a new phenomenon, its scale has increased with easier communication and faster international travel. Rapid transport is just one aspect of globalisation, which is defined by Anthony

Giddens (1990) as 'the intensification of worldwide social relations which link distant localities in such a way that local happenings are shaped by events occurring many miles away and vice versa'.

How does globalisation increase crime?

Some aspects of globalisation are crimogenic, making it difficult for national governments to control activities that originate outside their borders. The following crimes and inhumane practices are more likely to occur because of global inequalities and/or globalisation:

- illegal immigration, including transporting people by dangerous methods
- exploitation of immigrant workers (e.g. the Morecambe Bay cockle pickers, 2004)
- tricking migrant jobseekers into prostitution and abusing children sent to developed countries for education (e.g. Victoria Climbie, 2000)
- sex tourism
- sale of organs for transplants, and of children of desperately poor families for adoption
- internet pornography
- international terrorism
- smuggling of drugs, arms and endangered species
- exploitation by TNCs (companies operating in several countries) of workers and consumers in developing countries (e.g. the Nestlé baby milk controversy)
- pollution and dangerous practices in developing countries by TNCs (e.g. the Bhopal disaster, 1984)

The Union Carbide chemical plant at Bhopal

Task 5.6

Investigate the items in the list on page 85 and add recent examples, using the
internet and sources such as the world sociology unit of *Sociology for A2* (Moore,
Aiken and Chapman). Use the Wikipedia website to find the meaning of 'galamsey',
and then use the website below to find out about accusations against the mining
company Anglo Gold Ashanti and similar TNCs in Ghana.

www.minesandcommunities.org/Action/press672.htm

How can globalisation combat crime?

Easier global communications have encouraged the founding of international
organisations to combat shared problems, such as exploitation by TNCs, and
to protest against state crimes (acts by government agencies that break the state's
own criminal law or international law). State crimes include violation of human
rights, police corruption, torture, cover-up of environmental contamination,
tolerance of genocide and waging 'unjust' wars.

Task 5.7

Conduct a search for the following to decide whether or not they can be described as
state crimes:
- Lockerbie disaster, 1988
- imprisonment at Guantanamo Bay
- Camelford water scandal,1988
- Iraqi invasion of Kuwait, 1990
- massacres in Srebrenica, 1995
- Iraq War, 2003
- Abu Ghraib prisoner abuse
- extraordinary rendition of terrorist suspects
- Northwick Park hospital drugs trial, 2006

Guidance

Decide whether governments were responsible for, or are likely to have condoned,
the acts.

State–corporate crimes result from collusion between a state and a corporation. Green and Ward (2004) give the example of a developing nation so crippled
with debt repayment that it allows TNCs, offering prospects of capital growth,
to conduct business, despite breaking environmental and safety regulations.

Organisations that combat torture, imprisonment without trial and other human rights abuses include non-governmental organisations (NGOs) such as Amnesty International and international government organisations (IGOs) such as the United Nations Human Rights Council and the War Crimes Tribunal. Greenpeace has supporters worldwide and campaigns against environmental abuse and acts of aggression, even by the largest super power.

Box 5.1

Extracts from the Greenpeace website

After 2 years of investigation, we've uncovered a string of illegal soy production that is destroying the Amazon rainforest, and can be traced to a large American corporation: Cargill.

Activists from the *Esperanza* have climbed on board an illegal cargo vessel full of fish stolen from Guinean waters.

An exposé by respected insider journalist Seymour Hersh reveals that the USA is considering the use of tactical nuclear weapons against Iran. But where would those weapons come from, and where would they strike? Those questions bear deep implications for NATO and innocent civilians in Iran.

We have returned a large radioactive reminder of the Chernobyl disaster to the UN body pushing nuclear power. Radioactive soil was placed in the lobby of the International Atomic Energy Agency (IAEA) that has been trying to hide the consequences of the Chernobyl nuclear disaster.

Picpics/Alamy

The Greenpeace ship *Esperanza* moored in Cartagena, Spain

Despite the successes of Greenpeace, it is difficult to combat acts of deviance by companies that have branches in many countries and even harder for international organisations to prevent states from breaking agreements. North Korea recently withdrew from the Nuclear Non-proliferation Treaty and Iran appears to be trying to circumvent it, while a human rights crisis persists in Zimbabwe. Protest alone tends to have little effect; overthrowing leaders or imposing sanctions creates new problems. A controversial solution would be to create a world government, a political body more powerful than nation states. It would impose international law and tackle major problems, such as environmental degradation, that national governments could not solve independently.

Summary

- Words such as 'ethnicity', 'black' and 'Asian' need to be used carefully. Religious identity should not be overlooked because crime may be religiously or racially motivated.
- 'Asian' crime, viewed as insignificant until recently, has reached public attention as a result of riots and terrorism. It needs further research, as does heightened Islamophobia.
- Some ethnic groups are much more likely than whites to be stopped by police and to receive harsher punishments, despite the Macpherson recommendations.
- There are structural and other reasons why black Britons and other minorities may commit crime disproportionately, as well as becoming victims of crime more frequently.
- Global inequalities and aspects of globalisation give rise to some forms of crime.
- Easy global communication makes international action against crime and environmental degradation feasible, but it is still difficult in the absence of world government.

Task 5.8

Answer the following AQA question.

Identify and briefly explain:

(a) *one* way in which crime and deviance may be related to *one* of the following areas:
- education
- wealth, poverty and welfare
- work and leisure

(4 marks)

> ## Task 5.8 (continued)
>
> **(b)** *one* way in which crime and deviance may be related to *one* of the following areas:
> - power and politics
> - religion
> - world sociology   (4 marks)
>
> ### Guidance
> - Use headings to make it clear which option you have chosen in each part.
> - You could relate riots, such as those in Bradford, to any of the topics in **(a)** by identifying possible causes as educational failure, poverty or unemployment.
> - Terrorism could be a focus for any choice in **(b)**; drug smuggling or state crimes could be related to world sociology.
> - Avoid vague generalisation. In each case, inform your answer with references to sociologists, specific concepts such as globalisation, and theories such as left realism.

Useful websites

- Wikipedia on background to the Racial and Religious Hatred Act, 2006
  http://en.wikipedia.org/wiki/Racial_and_Religious_Hatred_Act_2006
- Summary of findings by the Commission on British Muslims and Islamophobia, 2004
  www.mcb.org.uk/library/Inayat-Islamophobia.pdf#search=%22Islamophobia%20report%22
- Home Office report, *Statistics on Race and the Criminal Justice System*, 2005
  www.homeoffice.gov.uk/rds/pdfs06/s95race05.pdf
- Wikipedia on state crime
  http://en.wikipedia.org/wiki/State_crime

Further reading

- Bowling, B. and Phillips, C. (2002) *Racism, Crime and Justice*, Pearson.
- Naim, M. (2006) *Illicit: How Smugglers, Traffickers and Copycats are Hijacking the Global Economy*, Heinemann.
- Rai, M. (2006) *7/7, the London Bombings, Islam and the Iraq War*, Pluto Press.
- Rowe, M. (2004) *Policing, Race and Racism*, Willan Publishing.
- Macey, M. 'Interpreting Islam: young Muslim men's involvement in criminal activity in Bradford', in B. Spalek (ed.) (2002) *Islam, Crime and Criminal Justice*, Willan Publishing.

Gender and crime

What issues of gender and crime are of current concern?

- Sociologists wish to discover whether the higher rate of crime by males, compared with that of females, reflects gender differences in activity or discrimination by the criminal justice system.
- Explanations are sought for recent increases in female crime, particularly by gangs of girls.
- There are disagreements about how frequently women are victims of male crimes, such as rape and domestic violence.
- Supporters of men's rights emphasise the degree to which men are victims of female violence and challenge the stereotype of the male as criminal.
- Feminists have discussed reasons why criminology has, until recently, been a male preserve and have suggested alternative methods of studying crime.

Note that crime and gender issues *relate synoptically to the family*.

Young women binge drinking

What are the patterns of offending by gender?

Recent Home Office research (*Statistics on Women and the Criminal Justice System, 2003*) found that:

- only 19% of known offenders and 6% of prisoners were women
- 14% of those being supervised by probation officers were female
- theft and handling were the most common indictable offences for women, accounting for 57% of the total
- 41% of female prisoners had been found guilty of drugs offences, 16% of violence against the person and 14% of theft and handling
- women 'grow out of crime'; their peak age of self-reported offending was 14 years and of recorded crime was 15 years, compared with 19 years for men.
- ethnic minority groups made up 29% of the female prison population, compared with 22% of the male equivalent
- 47% of females reported using crack cocaine in the year before going to prison and 57% took heroin, compared with 28% and 35% of males respectively
- 37% of women prisoners had previously attempted suicide; they were less likely than the general population to be in stable relationships but more likely to have childcare responsibilities
- 20% of women prisoners had experienced time in care
- the educational achievement of women prisoners was significantly lower than average

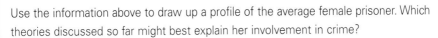

Task 6.1

Use the information above to draw up a profile of the average female prisoner. Which theories discussed so far might best explain her involvement in crime?

Guidance

Consider the theories of Merton (pp. 10–14) and Hirschi (pp. 16–17). Compare the results with subcultural explanations and left-wing theories.

Do the police and the courts discriminate against males?

Self-report studies suggest a higher proportion of females commit offences than are reflected by official statistics. Home Office figures cite 11% of females admitting to offences compared with 26% of males. Anne Campbell (1981) showed girls admitting to almost as many offences as boys in a male-to-female ratio of 1.2:1. However, her calculations were criticised for giving equal weight to trivial and serious offences.

Possible explanations for the discrepancy between self-reported female crime and relatively low official crime figures are that many female crimes, such as underage offences, are victimless, or are undetected because they are carried out 'invisibly' in the home. Such offences include prostitution, child abuse and elder abuse.

Alternatively, there is the chivalry thesis — police, magistrates and judges favour females, finding it difficult to believe that they are capable of behaving as badly as males.

Though Home Office figures reveal more lenient treatment for females, there may be reasons other than discrimination:

- Following arrest, women are more likely than men to be cautioned rather than charged. This partly reflects the fact that they admit more often to their crimes and may be arrested for less serious offences.
- Women are more likely than men to be discharged or given community sentences, as opposed to fines or prison sentences. On average, they receive shorter sentences — 71% receiving less than 1 year. According to the National Association for the Care and Resettlement of Offenders, judges are reluctant to give prison sentences to pregnant offenders or to those solely responsible for dependents. This results in gender differences in sentencing. Likewise, postnatal depression and premenstrual tension are sometimes regarded as mitigating circumstances.

On the other hand, in 2001, three men's jails were converted for use by women because female prisoner numbers had almost trebled in 6 years. This was attributed to increases in offences involving drugs and violence and to magistrates' deciding to get tougher on such crimes. Charlotte Day of the Howard League suggested the converse of the chivalry thesis:

> When a woman commits a crime, the courts are likely to view her as having trans-gressed not only legal law, but also the idea of feminine behaviour...so she's seen as even more deviant.
>
> Charlotte Day, the Howard League, 2001

Maggie Casburn (1985) also found courts to be harsher with female juveniles in cases of truancy, sexual promiscuity or resistance to family authority. There is a sexual double standard. Boys are expected to 'sow wild oats' but girls who do not conform to traditional moral codes are punished severely.

Are there reasons for genuinely lower offending rates by females?

The hormone testosterone is linked with aggression. However, of greater sociological significance is tolerance of male aggression by western societies. Socialisation of boys discourages displays of distress and promotes self-defence, reinforced by toys and media images that associate males with weaponry, taking risks and assertiveness. In contrast, females are still expected to be caring and gentler than males. When subject to pressure, they often become mentally ill and self-harm rather than attacking others, although instances in which women have killed chronically abusive partners show that this is not always the case.

James Q. Wilson suggested that:

> Young men are everywhere more likely than females or older persons to commit common street crimes, because of the way nature and nurture combine to make male children more impulsive and aggressive and less concerned with the well-being of others than females and adults.
>
> J. Q. Wilson, *Crime and Human Nature* (1985)

Conjugal role studies show that even employed women are expected to perform more domestic tasks than their partners and still take primary responsibility for childcare. This gives them less time to commit crime.

According to Frances Heidensohn (1985), single women are less likely than men to go to pubs or to be on the streets at night, where much crime is committed. This could indeed still be true for some Asian and middle-class schoolgirls. However, there is counter-evidence of widespread binge drinking by teenaged girls and of working-class, mid-teen girl gangs committing serious acts of violence, theft and robbery in, for example, London and Manchester. Nevertheless, younger girls may still spend much of their leisure in the bedroom subcultures described by Angela McRobbie (1978), whereas boys often collect in larger groups on the streets and may become involved in delinquency.

Some women lack the specific knowledge to commit certain types of crime, for example breaking into cars, and the physical strength and temperament for violence.

Corporate crimes are currently less likely to be committed by women. However, this may change as more women attain management positions.

Women's relative lack of earning power often motivates less spectacular crime. In her study of six women's prisons in England, Alexandra Mandaraka-Sheppard

(1986) found that a high proportion of the inmates had committed property crimes because they were in extreme financial difficulties and needed to be able to support their children.

Relative to male crime, why has female crime increased recently?

Freda Adler (1975) suggested that increasing gender equality has encouraged women into crime:

> It should come as no surprise that once women are armed with male opportunities they would endeavour to gain status, criminal as well as civil. The fact that woman is advancing so aptly into male positions strongly suggests that the old order rested much more on male cultural domination than on female genetic destiny.
>
> F. Adler, *Sisters in Crime: The Rise of the New Female Criminal* (1975)

Feminist attitudes may have encouraged girls to be more assertive and parents to supervise them less. However, Wilson (1985) disagreed:

> Rather than a modern woman rising in a previously male-dominated economy, the typical female offender has little sympathy for the women's movement.
>
> J. Q. Wilson, *Crime and Human Nature* (1985)

It is difficult to say whether media images of aggressive women reflect or contribute to changing attitudes. Increased availability of illegal drugs and the marketing of cheap alcohol to teenagers explain the growth of some types of female crime and victimisation. After binge drinking, the growth in female gangs has received most sociological attention. Anne Campbell interviewed girl-gang members in the UK (e.g. the Peckham Girls) for a *Public Eye* documentary in the late 1990s. She observed feisty attitudes, criminal activities and rituals, such as initiation ceremonies, that were similar to those of the American gangs described in her study *The Girls in the Gang: A Report from New York City* (1984).

In 1979, Campbell visited New York to study the roles of girls in street gangs. She spent 6 months researching the origins of American gangs, utilising key informants — for example, police and youth workers. (Note the *synoptic links with research methods*.) This pilot study provided background information.

American gangs are distinguished from friendship cliques by membership initiation, fixed roles, rules, names, 'colours', territoriality (often reflecting the ethnic identity of particular neighbourhoods), discipline, a philosophy and feuds with other gangs. Gang crimes, usually theft and fighting, provide a group solution to poverty and frustration in a country where no political party represents working class interests and trade unions are regarded as communist. New York male gangs, first recorded in the nineteenth century, often had female versions with complementary names, the members often consisting of girl friends or sisters of male gang members.

Until the 1970s, the few commentators who studied female gangs described girls' main roles as providing sex for the male gang and acting as lures to trick enemies into danger. They competed amongst themselves for male attention, resulting in 'cat fights'. A few were 'Good Girls', who married male gang members and made them give up their activities. The Tomboy, engaged in typical male activities of serious fighting, robbery, extortion, burglary and drug selling, was a rare figure.

Some researchers claim the roles of female gang members have changed in response to feminism and increased freedom from parental control. There is more sisterhood now within female gangs, status depends on respect of female peers and girls often remain after splitting with boyfriends in the companion gang. They wear trousers, boots, bandanas with the same gang insignia or 'colours' as the boys, and adopt assertive gang names like Battle Annie. Girls now fight in gang feuds and against police, increasingly using guns and knives.

For her main study, Campbell selected three female gangs — a racially mixed gang involved in burglary, robbery and drug dealing, a Puerto Rican biker gang dealing in drugs and prostitution and a black gang teaching Nation of Islam ideas, but which was also involved in crime. She spent 6 months carrying out participant observation with each gang, intensively interviewing a gatekeeper (key gang member) each time.

She had to reveal her purpose and used a tape recorder, except for discussing incriminating matters when respondents asked her to turn it off. As it is difficult to deceive observers over a long period, most of her impressions are probably valid.

> But there were, I do not doubt, facts that were hidden from me. Often accounts of criminal activities were oddly inconsistent over time: I suspect that on occasions members feared they had said too much and made attempts to cover themselves.
>
> A. Campbell, *The Girls in the Gang: A Report from New York City* (1984)

Their explanations were 'likely to be a function of their conceptions of themselves and the persons they wanted to present to me'.

The women were from poor immigrant backgrounds and had seen their mothers abused, evicted and rootless. They were determined to assume more control over their lives and the gang provided a substitute family. While they appeared to constitute a rebellious counterculture, they were traditionally feminine in their desires for pleasant apartments and loving husbands, and children were their main source of comfort. Some were married and all were dependent on men's love, though they were frequently let down by partners to whom promiscuity was part of a macho identity.

The gangs that Campbell studied typically existed as counterparts to male gangs; their uniforms and range of activities were dictated by men. They were allowed to fight, but were expected to be good wives and mothers.

> Though girls may occasionally defy them…the men remain indisputably in control.
> A. Campbell, *The Girls in the Gang: A Report from New York City* (1984)

Campbell disagreed with views that feminism has greatly changed women's criminal behaviour. She suggested that, far from being anarchic, the female gangs she encountered were surprisingly conventional, with pyramidal power structures of presidents and vice-presidents, initiation and promotion, thus reflecting patriarchal capitalist values.

Inevitably, Campbell's interpretation was subjective. Some of the behaviour she cited, such as a gang leader threatening with a knife a man who invited her to his apartment, was inconsistent with her overview that the women retained traditionally feminine attitudes.

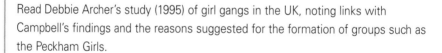

Task 6.2

Read Debbie Archer's study (1995) of girl gangs in the UK, noting links with Campbell's findings and the reasons suggested for the formation of groups such as the Peckham Girls.

Her paper for the British Criminology Conference (1995), 'Riot Grrrl and Raisin Girl: femininity within the female gang, the power of the popular', is on the internet: **www.britsoccrim.org/volume1/002.pdf#search=%22Riot%20Grrrl%20and%20 Raisin%20Girl%22**

Guidance

Archer suggests that A.K. Cohen's concept of status frustration is relevant, but emphasises changing gender role socialisation, observing that many female gang members have been brought up without fathers and adopt feisty roles in opposing men. Note the suggested influence of subcultures and products of popular culture such as punk, hip hop and riot grrrl.

Are patterns of victimisation gendered?

In the 1970s, radical feminists such as Kate Millett, Andrea Dworkin and Shulamith Firestone described the family as patriarchal, with men dominating their wives through domestic violence, rape and bullying, and imposing their surnames and wills on their wives and children. In *Sexual Politics* (1970), Millet suggested that patriarchy extends beyond the family to male doctors and to politicians making decisions about the availability of contraception and abortion. Susan Brownmiller drew attention to pornography and the media celebration of violence against women. 'Take Back the Night' marches were organised by feminist groups in the USA and western Europe to protest against the oppression of women in society and the media, and to assert their right to move freely in their communities by day and night without harassment and sexual assault.

Task 6.3

To what extent do the Home Office data below support assertions by radical feminists that rape and violence against women are highly prevalent and result from men's desire for control?

- According to Home Office research (2003), over 5% of adult men and almost 3% of women had been victims of violent crime in the previous 12 months.
- Men are the most frequent victims of stranger violence; women are more likely to know their attackers.
- Seventy-three per cent of domestic violence incidents were against women and 30% of homicide victims were female. Of female homicide victims, 46% were killed by current or former partners, compared with only 5% of men.
- According to British Crime Survey interviews, around one woman in 20 had been raped since the age of 16, with strangers accounting for only 8% of those rapes.
- Women, particularly young women, are more often stalked than men. The stalker is most likely to be someone known to them — usually an ex-partner.

Guidance

Note that most women know their assailants, whereas men are more often attacked by strangers, which suggests motives unconnected with family life.

Women fear street attacks and rape by strangers and, therefore, take precautions, but it is young men who are the prime targets for attack, usually by male assailants.

The statistics quoted in Task 6.3 are national averages. Local crime surveys, such as those in Merseyside and Islington that changed Jock Young's views, revealed high levels of crime suffered by the vulnerable poor in some inner-city areas. Women who were forced to go out on foot at night, for example some shift workers, were vulnerable to harassment, rape and bag snatching.

Furthermore, rape, harassment and domestic violence are under-reported by women. Women may be reluctant to report rape because of the persisting assumption that they misled the rapist by initially appearing to be willing. A campaign against the unethical treatment of rape victims in court resulted in new legislation in 2004, leading to the hope that more victims would press charges. However, recent media coverage of women whose testimonies were discounted because they had been drinking could act as a further disincentive.

There has been a 'male backlash' against feminist claims that women are frequent victims of male aggression. In *No More Sex War* (1992), Neil Lyndon described society as obsessed with women's rights and neglectful of those of men. As a result, women who commit crimes may be unsuspected, receive lighter sentences than men and be favoured in custody disputes. There is evidence that men are reluctant to admit to domestic attacks by female partners and there have been a few high-profile examples of jealous women slashing their husband's penis, such as the Bobbitt case in 1993.

Task 6.4

Compare the views and research data of pressure groups campaigning for greater justice for either men or women, including the following:

● Fawcett Society (Focus on: Women victims of violence)
  www.fawcettsociety.org.uk/index.asp?PageID=42
● UK Men and Fathers' Rights Website (Focus on: Criminal law)
  www.coeffic.demon.co.uk/descrim.htm#criminal_law
● Justice for Women — campaign for women who have killed or injured violent partners
  www.jfw.org.uk/ABOUTUS.HTM

Guidance

Consider how far points made on these sites can be trusted as accurate and objective. Is loaded language used? Is information selective?

Groups such as UK Men and Fathers' Rights point out that if a mother kills her baby of less than 1 year it is called infanticide and carries a lighter sentence than the same act by the father, which is described as murder. The reason for this is that mothers often act irrationally during severe postnatal depression. However, the point illustrates the view of some men that the law regards them as aggressive monsters less suited, than supposedly gentle women, to childcare.

Should feminists study crime differently?

Reasons for the lack of research into female subcultures are discussed in Chapter 4 (pp. 62–63). There are similar explanations for the shortage of studies of women offenders. Until recently, male sociologists dominated academic life. They were able to wander the 'mean' streets inhabited by criminals — areas traditionally off-limits to women researchers. However, there are feminist studies of female victims.

In *Women and Crime* (1985), Frances Heidensohn identified the most striking feature of crime statistics as the gender gap in offending patterns. She attributed this to men's control over women and girls. What female crime there is should be analysed within the context of family and gender roles and inequalities.

> Some groups of women have deliberately broken the law to expose the contradictions in the social and legal position of their sex and to make political statements. Others, constrained by socioeconomic pressures, commit crimes because alternative sources of income for them and their dependents are poor. For others, especially young girls, there will be subcultural pressures to conform to group or gang norms…The arena in which women's behaviour occurs will be similar for most groups of women…I am arguing for a perspective that is not…located in the sociology of deviance…but one which uses the analyses of family life, male dominance and separate spheres which feminist studies have to offer.
>
> F. Heidensohn, *Women and Crime* (1985)

Maria Mies (1993) argued that quantitative research disempowers the women studied, producing impersonal scientific data. Feminist research should be qualitative, so that the ideas of respondents are not forced into categories and the respondents should be as fully involved in the research as possible. Action research, in which sociologists and respondents collaborate, trying various solutions to problems such as domestic violence and monitoring their success, reflects these priorities.

In contrast, Maynard and Purvis (1994), in *Researching Women's Lives from a Feminist Perspective*, found quantification to be essential in discovering the extent and severity of violence against women and of crimogenic factors such as low pay. Early feminists preferred methods that involved warm human contact, but questionnaires can be effective by allowing the respondents anonymity when describing distressing experiences.

Postmodernist Carol Smart (1995) argued that gender is only one of many sources of identity and that crime cannot be defined easily. It is, therefore, pointless to conduct empirical research on the causes of male and female crime. Instead, she recommended discourse analysis — the examination of attitudes to female victims and offenders held by policemen, male judges and male-dominated media — to combat the oppression of women.

This debate between positivists, who base theories on hard data, and phenomenologists, sociologists interested in constructions of social phenomena such as crime, is well documented in the field of suicide and is discussed in Chapter 8. Smart's argument is interesting, but others would argue that, as crime rates are rising fast, there is continuing need for the use of all available research methods.

Summary

- Sociologists disagree about whether the higher rate of male crime is due to real gender differences or to discrimination against males by the criminal justice system.
- Crime by females has recently increased — particularly drug taking and gang activity, although Campbell did find some traditional gender attitudes in New York girl gangs.
- Home Office figures support feminist views that women are frequently victimised by male partners. However, young men are more often victims of stranger violence.
- Criminologists were, until recently, predominantly male. Feminists disagree about the best methods of studying gendered crime.

Task 6.5

Plan an answer to the following AQA question:

'Women are seen often only as the victims of crime. However, this is too simplistic a view of the relationship between gender and criminality.' Evaluate this view with reference to the alleged underrepresentation of women in crime statistics.

(40 marks)

Task 6.5 (continued)

Guidance
This question has a research methods emphasis and requires reference to the problems of official statistics and victim studies, outlined in Chapter 8, and to research about gendered crime:

- Begin by listing reasons why crime by females might be underestimated, including its relative invisibility and the chivalry thesis. Cite self-report studies and perhaps the views of men's groups to support this.
- Counter-argue with reasons why women may commit less crime than men, which is consistent with the official statistics.
- You might comment on the first sentence, suggesting that women are frequently crime victims, perhaps more often than they are offenders. Use Home Office and feminist research to support your case.
- Sum up by referring again to each part of the question.

Useful websites

- Home Office report, *Statistics on Women and the Criminal Justice System, 2003*
  www.homeoffice.gov.uk/rds/pdfs2/s95women03.pdf
- Wikipedia article on the 'Take Back the Night' movement
  en.wikipedia.org/wiki/Take_Back_the_Night

Further reading

- Campbell, A. (1984) *The Girls in the Gang: A Report from New York City*, Blackwell.
- Chesney-Lind, M. (2004) *The Female Offender*, Sage.
- Messerschmidt, J. (1993) *Masculinities and Crime*, Rowman and Littlefield.

Environmental and New Right theories

Why have urban areas become associated with crime?

Some parts of the UK suffer from much higher crime rates than others and people avoid certain areas because of their dangerous or seedy reputations. The extract in Box 7.1 gives just one example.

> Box 7.1
>
> St Ann's, and subsequently Nottingham itself, became infamous after the shooting of 14-year-old Danielle Beccan. Although there had already been numerous shootings on the estate, the murder of an innocent girl provoked understandable outrage, and drew attention to the ongoing gun and drug war between St Ann's and the Meadows, another inner-city Nottingham estate.
>
> **http://en.wikipedia.org/wiki/St_Anns**

TopFoto

Danielle Beccan

Why crime varies according to locality has interested sociologists since at least the nineteenth century. Recently, some of their theories have been embraced by New Right sociologists interested in situational crime prevention.

Until the industrial revolution, people probably felt safer in small towns than in the countryside, where they were vulnerable to highwaymen and footpads. There is a connection between the Latin word 'civis', meaning city dweller and words such as 'civilised' and 'civil', which reflects the Roman view that only people with developed social skills could live peaceably in large numbers.

In *The Problem of Crime* (2001), Peggotty Graham and John Clarke observed that by the mid-nineteenth century, cities were regarded as 'dangerous places', teeming with 'dangerous classes', the 'casual poor' or 'the 'social residuum'. Their 'rookeries' were likened to unexplored parts of the Empire, where the 'savages' needed 'taming'. Focus was on street and alley crimes; other types of urban crime such as financial fraud and domestic violence were overlooked. London exhibited striking class segregation; the West End glittered with commercial success and affluent leisure; the East End was associated with poverty, crime and 'aliens' from eastern Europe. 'The great unwashed' were feared as a health hazard to 'the great and the good'. They were considered to be an unruly mob swayed by revolutionary ideas — unprincipled people, whose marginal employment led to begging and crime. Respectable Victorians felt that these undesirables jeopardised national progress and that the speed at which they bred degraded the quality of the race. Such views can still be recognised in right-wing accounts of the feckless underclass on 'sink estates'.

Government attempts to address these problems included the creation of a modern police force, reconstruction of working-class areas for easier surveillance, sanitary improvements, restrictions on drinking, gambling, begging and prostitution, and promotion of 'rational' activities, such as temperance clubs.

In east London, the first university settlement was established at Toynbee Hall in 1884 by Samuel and Henrietta Barnett. It enabled academics to live alongside the urban poor to help solve their problems. They provided local people with free education and legal advice. The hall was a base for social researchers — for example, Charles Booth while working on *Life and Labour of the Poor in London* (1889–1902) and, later, William Beveridge, the founder of the Welfare State. After researching their needs, the university settlements helped the poor in other towns in a number of ways.

There were similar concerns in Paris about threats from the urban poor. In 1853, Baron Haussmann created wide boulevards that were harder for rebels to barricade.

The poor of London in 1875

Chapter 7

MAP DESCRIPTIVE OF LONDON POVERTY, 1898-9 (IN 12 SHEETS) — SHEET 5. EAST CENTRAL DISTRICT

Figure 7.1 Charles Booth's map of London poverty, 1898-99

THE STREETS ARE COLOURED ACCORDING TO THE GENERAL CONDITION OF THE INHABITANTS, AS UNDER:—

Lowest class. Vicious, semi-criminal. | Very poor, casual. Chronic want. | Poor. 18s. to 21s. a week for a moderate family. | Mixed. Some comfortable, others poor. | Fairly comfortable. Good ordinary earnings. | Middle class. Well-to-do. | NIL Upper-middle and Upper classes. Wealthy.

A combination of colours—as dark blue and black, or pink and red—indicates that the street contains a fair proportion of each of the classes represented by the respective colours.

Reproduced by permission of London School of Economics

104 Advanced **Topic**Master

How have environmental theories and urban initiatives developed since 1900?

In the twentieth century, the population drift to towns continued. Successful people sought pleasant living conditions in suburbs, leaving inner-city areas to the poor. Therefore, crime became associated with these depressed areas. This phenomenon also occurred in fast-growing US cities and became the subject of research at Chicago University.

In 1925, Robert Park and Ernest Burgess presented a model of a typical city as a series of concentric circles. From the centre, these are:

- Zone 1: central business district, few residents
- Zone 2: zone of transition, inhabited by the poor, new immigrants and temporary residents, with a few factories and small businesses
- Zone 3: respectable working-class district, including successful second-generation immigrants formerly from Zone 2
- Zone 4: middle-class suburbs
- Zone 5: wealthiest residents

Zones

1	Central business district (CBD)
2	Zone of transition
3	Residential (lower class)
4	Residential (middle class)
5	Residential (upper class)

Figure 7.2 Burgess's concentric ring model

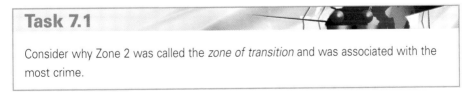

Task 7.1

Consider why Zone 2 was called the *zone of transition* and was associated with the most crime.

Park wrote, 'In the zone of deterioration encircling the central business section are always to be found the so-called "slums" and "badlands", with their submerged regions of poverty, and disease, and their underworlds of crime and vice'.

Residents of such areas included 'lost souls' in rented rooms, immigrants and Bohemians. Nowadays, the zone of transition is occupied frequently by students and poorer single parents. The zone has the lowest rents and is so called because once people's finances improve, they move out.

Shaw and McKay (1929), also of the 'Chicago School', built on this work by demonstrating that a high proportion of Chicago's juvenile delinquents lived in this zone. Their arguments are probably true of such areas today.

Why is the level of crime high in zones of transition?

Crime rates are high because:

- the residents' poverty motivates local property crimes, drug dealing and prostitution. According to P. J. and P. L. Brantingham's more recent theory of cognitive maps (1984), opportunist offenders commit crimes along familiar local routes.
- residents live there temporarily and often have little in common, so schemes such as Neighbourhood Watch are rarely organised
- residents do not recognise their neighbours, so they are unlikely to notice intruders
- residents are less able to afford burglar alarms and personal transport, so are vulnerable to burglary and attack
- housing space is restricted, so there is a street corner culture, which encourages delinquency

This ecological theory (relating to environmental effects) links with subcultural studies because cultural heterogeneity (different backgrounds) and the area's social disorganisation reduce the likelihood of the young being socialised into mainstream values. In fact, according to Shaw and McKay's later cultural transmission theory (1942), deviant values might become the norm in such areas. Sutherland and Cressey (1954) suggested that the likelihood of such factors influencing local residents might be predicted by examining factors such as age, how long they have lived in the area, the prestige of local criminals and how often they are encountered. This is the concept of differential association.

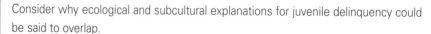

Task 7.2

Consider why ecological and subcultural explanations for juvenile delinquency could be said to overlap.

Guidance

Look back at the earlier subcultural theories and see how many relate to gatherings of local youths.

Graham and Clarke (2001) suggested that as the British public travelled through similar zones of transition on the way to the central business district, sights of street-corner youths increased their fears of inner-city delinquency. In the 1950s, the government's 'belief in the transformative power of the built environment' resulted in former slum-dwellers being rehoused in New Towns and suburban housing estates.

Why did inner-city problems persist?

By the 1970s, it was clear that inner-city problems had not disappeared. While many families had been rehoused, the elderly and the young, unable to afford council house rents or mortgages, had not. They remained in the deteriorating inner cities and were joined by Commonwealth immigrants, who also needed cheap accommodation. Poorly integrated communities resulted, blighted by fears of racist attacks and muggings, with the host population being outnumbered by outsiders, as documented by Hall (see Chapter 4, p. 64).

Well-meaning attempts to 'reclaim' inner-city areas encouraged middle-class people to buy 'gentrified property'. This made some inner-city areas feel safer but created greater problems for the poor as they competed for inferior housing in worse areas. Policy makers began to realise that there would always be people too deprived to take advantage of new housing initiatives, posing a permanent threat of inner-city crime. During the 1970s and 80s, reported crime increased and clear-up rates went down. This put pressure on the police and made them keener to stop-and-search people from ethnic minorities on suspicion. Overuse of this tactic — for example, Operation Swamp, conducted by police in Brixton in 1981 to combat street crime — generated resentment among the black population, which erupted into riots that year and in similar circumstances in 1985.

What caused housing estate crime?

While inner-city problems persisted, crime rates were not easily reduced among those moved out to better housing, particularly where many 'problem families' were settled together. Traditional communities and supportive, extended families had been fragmented by rehousing. In 1991, economically deprived young males from housing estates on the outskirts of Cardiff and Oxford and on Tyneside expressed their frustration by stealing and burning cars, wreaking havoc against neighbours and fighting police. Media attention shifted temporarily from the inner cities to housing estates as crime hot spots. The American New Right commentator Charles Murray blamed the high proportion of disorganised and single-parent families.

What is 'Fortress Britain'?

Reasons behind the 2001 riots in Bradford and other northern towns have been discussed. At the other end of the social scale, through fear of crime, prosperous citizens in 'Fortress Britain' have opted increasingly to live in secure settings — for example, behind electronically controlled gates or in flats where only residents and identified acquaintances can gain access. In America, gated communities are common, with access to 'public' spaces nearby made difficult for non-residents because of parking restrictions. Benches fitted with sprayers discourage sleepers, and undesirables are ejected from shopping malls. In her novel *Oryx and Crake* (2003), Margaret Atwood describes a futuristic society in which respectables live in locked communities away from social outcasts and venture out at extreme peril. Some sociologists argue that right-wing labelling of the underclass, reminiscent of Victorian fears of the 'social residuum', could result in extremes of social segregation, not unlike Atwood's scenario.

A new estate in Surrey — an example of 'Fortress Britain'?

How do New Right theorists explain crime?

The term New Right refers to conservative thinkers whose ideas have developed from consensus perspectives such as that of Durkheim. Although they differ on some issues, they agree that the laws upheld in society are sound and benefit the majority. Unlike Marxists and social constructionists, they accept capitalism as desirable and the power of the criminal justice system as even-handed. In general, crime is viewed as selfish and immoral, and punishment as justifiable.

They are sometimes known as **Right realists** since, like Left realists, they focus on the need to reduce the currently increasing crime rates. However, the reasons they suggest for crime and its solutions contrast starkly with those of Left realists. Some of their key ideas are expressed in *Crime and Human Nature* (1985), by James Q. Wilson and Richard Herrnstein.

Man the calculator

The rational choice theory originates from the view of the philosophers Thomas Hobbes and Jeremy Bentham that man is naturally desirous of material gain but accepts the rule of law in order to be protected from others. The attempts of a determined few to selfishly pursue their own ends can be discouraged by punishments that just outweigh the benefits of each offence. Excessive, vengeful punishments are inefficient and may encourage people to try to overthrow the system.

This view is at odds with the assumption by conservatives that the harsher the punishment, the more effective the deterrent. Wilson and Herrnstein observed that, 'It may be easier to reduce crime by making penalties swifter and more certain rather than more severe, if the persons committing crime are highly present-oriented'.

Psychological and biological factors

The theory is complicated by the fact that not everyone is equally rational. Leaving aside the mentally ill, some people are poorer at anticipating the results of their actions and some, particularly males, enjoy risk taking, according to Wilson and Herrnstein. Unlike crime theories explored in earlier chapters, New Right perspectives incorporate psychological as well as social explanations. The suggestion is that aspects of genetic inheritance, such as aggression, intelligence, extroversion, impulsiveness, hyperactivity and empathy, as well as age, affect decisions about whether or not to commit crime, although there is no 'crime gene'.

Other biological factors, such as the chromosomal aberration XYY, which is associated with low intelligence, and oxygen starvation at birth, may also affect the predisposition towards crime. Criminal behaviour is a product of both genetic and environmental factors. Their relative importance has yet to be determined and more longitudinal research is needed.

We do know enough to be fairly confident that criminal behaviour cannot be explained wholly by reference to the social circumstances in which an individual finds herself or himself.

J.Q. Wilson and R. Herrnstein, Crime and Human Nature (1985)

This means that social policies can never totally eradicate crime.

Is youth a crucial factor?

Further support for the inevitability of crime is the evidence that, regardless of the society, youth in itself is crimogenic.

> The rise in crime at puberty accompanies the awakening of major sources of reinforcement for delinquent behaviour — money, sex, and peers who value independence of, or even defiance of, conventional morality. At the same time, the growing child is literally, as well as psychologically, independent of powerful adults (parents, etc.) who might reinforce conventional standards. Given energy, strength, potent new sources of drive but few legitimate means of consummation, a lack of economic and social skills, and peers who are similarly vigorous and frustrated, the adolescent years are destined to foster a rise in delinquency. Self-report studies confirm that almost all teenagers, 90% or more in some populations, commit at least one criminal offence.
>
> J.Q. Wilson and R. Herrnstein, Crime and Human Nature (1985)

Adults often have easier access to legitimate sources of money, sex and status, are more likely to have developed responsibilities, ties and principled guidelines for action, and have extended time horizons, that is, they are better able to defer gratification. As people age, their 'drives cool off'.

Is family socialisation important?

Durkheim stressed the importance of early upbringing, so that morality becomes internalised as the collective conscience. Likewise, Wilson and Herrnstein observed that, as well as calculating the risks and benefits of crime, most people are 'governed by conscience, sympathy and a sense of justice' that inhibits crime when adequate socialisation has occurred within stable families. Closely bonded people wish to retain the good opinion of family, friends and employers, as Hirschi also suggested.

Unlike Murray, Wilson and Herrnstein conceded that there is a lack of clear evidence associating children of single-parent families or even abusive families with crime, although this is likely to impede effective socialisation.

> The central features of family life — a fortunate biological endowment, secure attachments and consistent discipline — are more important than whether it is a two-parent family, one with a working mother, or one in which corporal punishment is frequently employed.
>
> J.Q. Wilson and R. Herrnstein, Crime and Human Nature (1985)

They cited research by Werner and Smith that suggests that forming a close bond with the mother in the first year or two of life, being the firstborn and growing up in a family of four or fewer children, are factors that correlate with children's ability to cope with other stresses of life without becoming delinquent.

Are media and alcohol crimogenic?

Wilson and Herrnstein took the popular view that mass media, particularly television, may increase aggression, as well as making viewers more aware of social inequities, thus increasing the motivation for crime. Alcohol also generates crime by making people more aggressive and impulsive.

Task 7.3

Many social scientists question whether links between screen violence and real violence can be proved. Read about the uses and gratifications theory and other media-effect theories to form your own opinion.

Does relative poverty cause crime?

Although unemployment often correlates with crime, Wilson and Herrnstein cited American and British longitudinal research that indicates that negative early attitudes may well be the cause of both. For example, West and Farrington found that many delinquents had done poorly at school, adopted an anti-authority stance, lacked motivation and were indifferent about work. Therefore, a poor economy cannot necessarily be held responsible for increasing crime, and general affluence may improve opportunities for offending. Wilson and Herrnstein found no conclusive evidence that a sense of relative deprivation increases property crime — it correlates more closely with assault and homicide against equally deprived acquaintances.

Right libertarianism

Other New Right thinkers have developed this position to oppose job creation and the extension of welfare benefits. For example, Milton Friedman (1980) argued that welfare provision should be reduced because state support discourages people from taking responsibility for themselves and family members, with demoralising effects. Workers resent paying taxes to support a welfare system and may be tempted to evade tax and then go down the slippery slope to commit other offences. Similarly, in *Anarchy, State and Utopia* (1974), Robert Nozick described income tax as theft by the state. He felt it was wrong that those who gave up leisure to work long hours should also have to give up their earnings through tax while the unemployed gained both leisure and welfare benefits. Thus, some New Right thinkers believe that:

- the state should intervene as little as possible in the lives of citizens
- there should be a minimum number of laws
- people should be allowed to pursue their own interests so long as they do not harm others

This is known as libertarianism.

Task 7.4

What do you think would be the practical and ethical problems of reducing welfare benefits in the hope of cutting crime?

Guidance

Marxists and left realists believe poverty is a cause of crime.

Why is the level of crime increasing?

If crime rates go up, it is difficult to disentangle the relative influences of the proportion of people committing crime (prevalence) from the number of offences criminals commit (incidence) and the lengths of criminal careers (increases or decreases in the years individuals are criminally active). Wilson and Herrnstein were concerned by increases in the level of crime in the USA and western Europe since the mid-twentieth century. They suggested that long-term changes reflect three factors:

- **The proportion of young males in the population**
- **Changes in the benefits and costs of crime** Urbanisation inevitably increases opportunities for theft and burglary and, as more valuable portable goods became available, the crime rate increased. Changes in the costs of crime relate to the risk and harshness of punishment, for example, whether imprisonment is likely, and to the relative attractiveness of employment, staying at school or an idle life supported by welfare benefits and crime.
- **The level of society's investment in instilling an internalised commitment to self-control via families, local communities, schools, religious organisations and the media** It is possible that permissive parents have tolerated impulsiveness and present-time orientation in children.

Crime rates are unusually low in nations like Japan, where the norms inculcated by the family and general culture emphasise obligations more than rights and where families transmit a sense of collective responsibility for behaviour.

J.Q. Wilson and R. Herrnstein, *Crime and Human Nature* (1985)

Reduced church attendance and the decline of Sunday Schools and organisations that encourage self-control, such as the temperance movement, mean that children are less likely to absorb moral principles outside the home.

Note the *synoptic links here with religion, the family, and wealth, welfare and poverty.*

Task 7.5

Of the three factors suggested by Wilson and Herrnstein as being responsible for changing crime rates, which could most easily be influenced by social policies?

Guidance

Consider target-hardening initiatives to increase the difficulties of committing crime, Neighbourhood Watch, imprisonment for lesser offences and the use of ASBOs. Parenting classes and the study of citizenship in schools are attempts to encourage self-control.

Strengthening of moral codes

Wilson and Herrnstein argued that the three factors above are more significant than economic recession or affluence. The evidence is that the 1960s and 1970s saw an increase not only in crime but in 'other social pathologies' — for example, suicide, divorce, illegitimate births, alcohol and drug abuse and football hooliganism. It is hard to relate these to economic problems, but all are consistent with changes in families and cultural attitudes. Therefore, it is logical to also explain crime this way.

This view has much in common with paternalist conservatives such as Ernest van den Haag (1975), Stephen Davies (1987) and Christie Davies (1992). All stress the need for traditional attitudes of personal responsibility and decency. Governments should improve the moral climate by discouraging pornography, the sex trade, substance abuse and general permissiveness. In contrast to libertarians, paternalists believe there should be *more* laws rather than fewer. Some advocate zero tolerance — discouragement by the police and community wardens of public acts that are not necessarily illegal but which depress the moral tone of an area, such as drinking in the street, loitering and sleeping in doorways. The term paternalism denotes the adoption by the legislature of the role of a caring parent, discouraging the vulnerable from harming themselves. Laws concerning the wearing of seat belts, food safety and age-related regulations for harmful and addictive substances are condemned by opponents as symptomatic of the 'nanny state'.

Decline of the traditional family

Some writers express more certainty than Wilson and Herrnstein that the decline in two-parent families is a reason that children are 'out of control'. Charles Murray, for example, blamed crime on housing estates to the high proportion of disorganised and single-parent families. In *Rising Crime and the Dismembered Family* (1993), Norman Dennis condemned political correctness for its denial that the family is breaking down, with disastrous consequences for wider society. Both writers attributed delinquency to the absence in households of responsible fathers. They put the blame less on divorce than on never-married parents. Increasing numbers of children are the result of either brief cohabitation or the willingness of working-class girls to have children by unemployed men whom they are unwilling to marry, perhaps in the hope of obtaining council flats.

Boys that grow up in such circumstances lack the daily role model of a responsible, breadwinning father. Their socialisation and supervision by a young mother may be inadequate, thus increasing the likelihood of them copying the delinquent activities of older boys.

A *Sunday Times* article by Robert Winnett in 2005 shows that fears of a growing delinquent underclass are still prevalent. It condemns 'Neets' — people not in employment, education or training and claiming benefits — as a 'social tribe gnawing away at Britain's values and resources'. Their children 'have never been socialised and they simply don't know how to behave, from sitting still in classrooms to knowing you don't hit people if you have a problem'.

Law enforcement

Wilson and Herrnstein argued that, although criminal behaviour may partly result from inherited qualities or childhood conditions, it must still be punished. A lax system of law will fail to satisfy the public desire for justice, will risk vigilantism and tempt more potential offenders.

> When we punish offenders, we hope to prevent them from offending again and to deter like-minded people from committing similar offences. But we are also reaffirming the moral order of society and reminding people of what constitutes right conduct, in hopes that this reaffirmation and reminder will help people, especially in families, teach each other about virtue.
>
> J.Q. Wilson and R. Herrnstein, *Crime and Human Nature* (1985)

Administrative criminology

Some current criminologists are much less interested than Wilson and Herrnstein in human issues such as 'virtue' and simply wish to reduce crime through practical measures ('administration'), drawing on environmental theories and data. According to research by Baldwin and Bottoms (1976), further developed by Skogan (1990), areas can easily 'tip' into crime if they are allowed to deteriorate physically and if social disorder, such as alcohol and drug abuse, is tolerated on the streets. 'Respectables' move away and no longer visit the area for leisure purposes. Therefore, fewer law-abiding people are walking the streets and those who remain are vulnerable to attack. As the reputation of the area falls, house prices plummet, speculators buy property for multi-occupation and the area becomes a crime-prone zone of transition. Areas beginning to 'tip' can sometimes be rescued by zero tolerance policing and local authority measures, such as financial inducements to professionals to move in.

Attention has also been paid to 'designing out crime' on housing estates by eliminating features such as tunnels, walkways that allow easy access to upper storeys, and ill-lit areas where offenders can hide.

Fraser Brown Newman Architects

The rejuvenated West Granton estate, Edinburgh

There has been recent research into minimising the likelihood of crime occurring in specific places. In an article in *Rational Choice and Situational Crime Prevention* (1997), Nick Tilley cited the proverb, 'Even the bishop is tempted by the open strong box'. Target hardening can discourage most potential offenders, who are opportunists, from committing crime on impulse. Only the most determined will try again in less protected areas elsewhere (displacement). Tilley observed that, 'an offence takes place when the adequately motivated offender meets the sufficiently suitable target, in the absence of plausible enough guardianship or sufficiently salient handling'.

Note that:

- a handler means someone who might deflect the offender, such as a parent, community warden or passer-by
- a guardian refers to a security guard, police officer or device such as an alarm or CCTV camera

Supporters of situational crime prevention believe, therefore, that crime can be reduced if property owners can be encouraged to invest in effective locks and alarms and to keep their goods out of sight, and if there is maximum surveillance of public spaces.

What are the shortcomings of New Right arguments?

- There is little attempt to explore the social causes of crime. Administrative criminologists in particular are uninterested in criminal motivation, so their work can scarcely be described as sociology. Even Wilson and Herrnstein, although they discuss many possibilities, are more interested in correlations between crime and psychological and biological factors, rather than social causes.
- Economic explanations for crime are ignored, except to acknowledge that, in a competitive society, it is inevitable that less successful people will be tempted into property crime. Marxists and left realists would deplore the lack of interest in reducing poverty and social exclusion.
- Suggestions that welfare benefits should be cut are both inhumane and impractical.
- Assumptions are made that laws are sound and enforced fairly by the criminal justice system, with no acknowledgement that crime statistics might be biased.
- Libertarian ideas that people should be allowed to commit acts that harm only themselves seem callous, and zero tolerance policies are equally problematical. If the police are allowed to target those whose behaviour is not illegal but simply antisocial, powerless groups are likely to feel harassed.

Summary

- Since the drift of population away from the countryside during the industrial revolution, towns have become associated with crime.
- The Chicago school environmental theories identified the zone of transition as being particularly prone to social disorganisation and crime.
- Attempts in Britain to reduce working-class crime by building out-of-town public housing estates were generally unsuccessful. Inner-city crime continued while estate riots drew attention to a growing underclass.
- New Right arguments are based on consensus theories, accepting laws as the will of the majority.
- In a competitive society, unless it is made less attractive to them by target hardening and the likelihood of punishment, less successful people will make the rational choice to commit crime.
- Socialisation in the traditional family should teach people to take responsibility for their actions. However, youth and individual differences make some crime inevitable.
- Libertarians and paternalists differ as to the extent to which the government should punish victimless crimes or practise zero tolerance.
- Left-wingers criticise the New Right for their lack of sympathy for the poor and marginalised.

Task 7.6

Make notes in response to the following question, adapted from AQA.

Examine some of the problems involved in using statistics to measure crime in different areas. (12 marks)

Guidance

Prepare for this question by reading about the problems with official crime statistics and results of national and local victim surveys — for example, in Stephen Moore's *Investigating Crime and Deviance*.

- Police statistics for inner cities and public housing estates may be higher than for other areas not only because of a higher level of crime but because of police patrolling patterns. Police are more likely to stop and search people in these areas. Therefore, they will uncover more offences.
- On the other hand, victim surveys show that people in the most crime-prone areas are least likely to report crimes to the police, through lack of faith in their effectiveness and fairness, and through fear of reprisals. The Merseyside and Islington Crime Surveys revealed that certain types of crime that occur frequently in

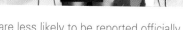

Task 7.6 (continued)

inner-city areas, for example rape and assault, are less likely to be reported officially than other crimes, such as car theft.

- In remote rural areas, some victimless crimes go unnoticed and are, therefore, unreported. Laws relating to the sale of alcohol are routinely flouted. Under-policing in such areas means that police uncover fewer crimes. It also discourages people from reporting minor crimes; a Home Office survey (2000) estimated the true level in some areas to be six times greater than reported. Community police in the countryside are more likely to give informal warnings to locals; city police may press charges against strangers.
- On the other hand, crime levels in villages may be lower because people keep an eye on neighbours' property, notice strangers and know where local suspects live.

Research suggestions

- Ask adults if they have been victims of property crime and, if so, whether they subsequently received advice from the police on target hardening. What suggestions for situational crime prevention are made on the police website for your locality?
- Consider whether there is a zone of transition in your local town. Read the crime reports in your local newspaper and on the police website to see whether a disproportionate amount of crime occurs there.
- Ask people whether any local areas are **tipping** and then, in safe conditions with a friend, visit the areas to note typical signs of the process occurring. Consult local council websites to see if steps are being taken to 'rescue' the area.

Useful websites

- Account of local gang rivalries in Nottingham
  http://news.bbc.co.uk/1/hi/england/nottinghamshire/4327066.stm
- Home Office report on situational crime prevention
  www.homeoffice.gov.uk/rds/prgpdfs/crrs11.pdf
- Student notes on theoretical perspectives (Focus on: New Right)
  www.sociology.org.uk/cardthy1.htm

Further reading

- Moore, S. (1996) *Investigating Crime and Deviance*, Collins.
- Muncie, J. and McLaughlin, E. (2001) *The Problem of Crime*, Sage.
- Wilson, J. and Herrnstein, R. (1985) *Crime and Human Nature*, Simon and Schuster.

Researching crime and deviance

Crime is one of the most fascinating but difficult areas for researchers to study. Many of the problems have already been discussed, so the purpose of this chapter is to draw the threads together, expand some points and finally compare different approaches to a particular form of deviance — suicide.

What are the problems of primary methods?

Primary methods, such as interviews, questionnaires, observation and experiments, involve the researcher in generating new data. Becker (1963) identified some methodological problems.

- Not all deviants are caught and some are falsely accused. Therefore, questions to those labelled as deviants will produce skewed data, focusing on the traits of the least successful and least powerful of potential deviants.
- Theories should not be built on only a small number of cases and it is difficult to identify and access deviants because their activities tend to be hidden. This problem and the one above relate to the need for representative (typical) data.
- Researchers have to spend time gaining the trust of deviants, reassuring them that they will not suffer for what they reveal. This may involve keeping unusual hours and changing lifestyle, which is a practical problem.
- Deviance within powerful organisations will be hidden carefully. Investigators need permission to enter business, medical or educational organisations to conduct research. If managers allow this, they will limit the area of enquiry to maintain secrecy. Thus, there is a problem of access.
- Empathising with the perspective of the deviant group (verstehen, as Weber called it) is impossible as an objective observer. In order to fully understand their norms and values, researchers must — despite moral qualms — immerse themselves in the lifestyle of the group. Obtaining valid data (reflecting the truth) may create ethical problems.

- It will subsequently be difficult to join an opposing group, for example law enforcers, and gain their trust sufficiently to seek valid information from them and absorb their viewpoint fully enough to be able to describe it. Yet reporting on both law-breakers and law-makers is necessary for interactionist studies. This relates to the need for objectivity (providing a neutral and balanced account).

The ethical concerns that feminists have about sensitive ways of studying victims so that they feel involved, rather than used, have already been discussed. Other ethical problems relate to confidentiality:

- Researchers wish to present a detailed account of their findings without their subjects being recognised,
- There is a possibility of becoming involved in the group's criminal activity.
- When researchers have to hide their identities or purpose, there is the ethical dilemma of deception.

Practical problems of covert observation include gaining access to a group through acquiring a suitable native costume (looking the part) or entry via a gatekeeper. There may be elements of danger if criminals being covertly observed realise the researcher's intentions. Making notes on the spot is therefore likely to be impossible.

What are the relative advantages of primary and secondary methods?

Primary methods enable sociologists to meet people at first hand or, in the case of questionnaires, to ask respondents exactly what they wish to find out. This is more flexible than having to rely on secondary (pre-existing) data such as media accounts, textbooks, historical documents and official statistics. Researchers intrigued to find the causes of recent events will find little secondary data available.

Secondary data may be selective, dated or unreliable (written from a particular viewpoint) and their validity is difficult to check. By seeking primary data, the researcher is more in control and may find more human interest.

On the other hand, secondary data, such as official statistics, are accessible and present a fuller picture than a researcher could possibly discover by accessing individuals. They provide a useful starting point, allowing comparisons between groups over time, and raising interesting questions.

Media accounts and historical documents allow access to past or distant events; textbooks and academic articles provide useful background. These sources need careful interpretation and are unlikely to answer all the researcher's questions.

> ## Task 8.1
>
> - Look over the detailed accounts in earlier chapters of the primary methods used by Rosenhan, Wing (pp. 41–43), and Anne Campbell (pp. 94–96), making notes of their strengths and weaknesses.
> - Do you regard the semiology practised by the CCCS as a primary or secondary method? This depends on whether they observed youths at first hand or media images of them (pp. 58–62).
> - Check that you have notes on the secondary methods of media and statistical analysis employed by Hall in *Policing the Crisis* (pp. 64–65).

Why do sociologists use several methods?

Virtually all sociologists access previous work on their topic and talk informally to relevant people. However, some make a point of triangulating (using more than one main method). This can be used:

- to offset the limitations of each method by using the strengths of the others
- for comparison purposes

To gain insight into labelling, Stanley Cohen compared media accounts of mods and rockers with primary data from interviews and observation. Likewise, Jock Young contrasted media exaggeration of drug taking with his own observations.

What are the problems of using official statistics?

Previous chapters have identified why official statistics relating to differences of gender, ethnicity or locality may be flawed. Marxist and subculturalists argue that street crime and offences by working-class youths are reported, while corporate and white-collar crimes by higher-class, middle-aged 'respectables' may escape notice. Prison statistics and figures for fines and cautions may indicate more about the operations of the criminal justice system than about patterns of offending.

Why are crimes not reported?

Public failure to report crime has already been covered. Reasons include:
- fear of reprisals
- lack of faith in, or easy access to, the police

- embarrassment
- when no gain, such as compensation from insurance, is expected
- protection of the perpetrator
- the trivial nature of many offences

Why are crimes not recorded?

Crimes that are not reported by the public are only uncovered by police if they visit the relevant area — patterns of patrolling, and stop-and-searches are irregular. In addition, particular police forces have priorities and minor offences not fitting into these categories may be ignored. It is only practical to record and process a limited number of cases. Police may dissuade victims of minor offences from pursuing the matter by asking for a written statement. Reports from unreliable witnesses may receive little attention. However, some instances, for example allegedly racist incidents, must now be recorded. Police discretion allows them to overlook small incidents where the perpetrator is apologetic, while to maintain their authority, they record similar acts by confrontational offenders.

How useful are victim surveys?

Every year, for the British Crime Survey, a representative sample of the public are interviewed about crimes of which they have been victims. Media stories about crime rates now cite these data alongside official police statistics and Home Office reports use the findings. Victims reluctant to report offences to the police may be more willing to do so to researchers. However, there are short-comings:
- Corporate, white-collar and victimless crimes are omitted.
- Embarrassing crimes, for example rape, are still under-reported.
- Under-16s are not asked; therefore, child abuse is excluded.
- Memories may be faulty.
- Multiple experiences of the same crime may not show up.
- The national averages produced by the British Crime Survey mask the high incidence of victimisation for particular types of people in particular areas. Local victim surveys reflect these differences more accurately.

How useful are self-report studies?

Many illegal acts, such as underage offences, are victimless; others remain undiscovered by victims. Self-report studies can be used to uncover such offences and are useful when comparing groups — for example, Campbell's study of the patterns of offending of boys and girls.

Contrasting self-report studies with police or prison statistics may suggest that particular groups are treated more leniently by the criminal justice system. Problems are as follows:

- Respondents are only likely to admit to offences when it is clear that their questionnaires will be collected as part of a large anonymous group. The method is therefore limited to use in institutions such as schools and colleges.
- Validity may be low. Respondents may not admit to serious crimes or they may make false claims to look 'cool'.
- Questions only ask whether the listed offences have been committed, not why. The results are therefore shallow, generating statistics without motives.
- It is difficult to devise a counting system that distinguishes serious from minor offences.

What is the most effective method of studying suicide?

When assessing a particular research method it is helpful to use three criteria: practical, ethical and theoretical (easily remembered by the mnemonic PET). Focus so far has been on practical and ethical problems, but we now turn to theoretical issues. In Chapter 6, feminist views of the relative merits of using quantitative (positivist or scientific) or qualitative (interpretive) methods for studying crime and victimisation were discussed. The same debate has been conducted over suicide research. The many reasons for suicide are well covered in specialist books; there is only space here to focus on why it is so difficult to research.

Durkheim's approach to suicide

Durkheim was interested in suicide because he noticed that suicide rates varied between different nations, yet, unless there were major societal changes, the rate in each individual nation remained stable year after year. This suggested that the apparently individualistic decision to attempt suicide is actually a response to social forces. Studying these data scientifically could increase understanding of how societies malfunctioned, in the hope of reducing deviance such as suicide.

The scientific method

Durkheim broadly followed the steps of the scientific method:
- Preliminary observations generate a hypothesis.

- The sociologist decides on the kind of findings that would support the hypothesis and operationalises these outcomes as phenomena that can be accurately identified and measured (empirical data).
- The effects of different variables that might affect the outcome are controlled and the variables are manipulated.
- The results are objectively compared with the hypothesis to see if they support it.
- If there is doubt, tests continue, perhaps using a modified hypothesis.

Unable to observe the suicide phenomenon itself, Durkheim instead conducted multi-variate analysis of suicide rates. He collected international statistics and the social characteristics of the victims, for example religion, age, sex, social class and locality, so that he could look for correlations and compare groups. He regarded suicide statistics as 'social facts', which could be studied in the same way as scientific facts.

Durkheim's realist approach

As a structuralist, Durkheim tried to link suicide rates of different religious groups such as Protestants and Catholics with broader concepts such as social cohesion and social regulation. These are harder to identify and measure empirically, so positivists disapproved of this aspect of his research. Strictly speaking, therefore, he was not a positivist, but a realist — a sociologist interested in statistics but conscious of their limitations and willing to investigate interesting, less easily measurable, phenomena. Positivists particularly criticised Durkheim's assumption that suicide rates in Catholic areas of Germany were low because Catholicism encourages social cohesion; the rates may have been low because Catholic coroners were reluctant to classify deaths as suicide or because the areas were rural. Durkheim was unable to eliminate all variables, yet his work is still of interest.

Followers of Durkheim's methods

Despite the above criticisms, many sociologists have continued to investigate suicide by studying correlations. Halbwachs (1930) found it to be lower in rural than in urban areas and suggested the impersonal nature of town life as an explanation. Similarly, Sainsbury (1955) found a positive correlation between suicide rates and social isolation in a comparison between London boroughs.

Contemporary research is often based on statistics. Childline keeps records of the sex and family circumstances of those who telephone for help. In 2001, McClure observed that the rate of suicide in 15–19-year-old males almost doubled between 1970 and 1990. He conceded that the figures were probably underestimated because coroners prefer to classify unexplained deaths as 'undetermined or accidental'. However, such apparent trends are too striking to be ignored.

Phenomenological approaches to suicide

Durkheim's methods are only sound if the statistics used are correct. Interpretivists are sceptical about the validity of suicide statistics and as part of this approach, phenomenologists (sociologists interested in how people view particular aspects of society) have undertaken studies to show that suicide statistics are social constructions made by coroners.

Atkinson, Kessel and Daalgard in *The Comparability of Suicide Rates* (1975) conducted an experiment in which they asked four English and five Danish coroners to reach verdicts on the same 40 cases. The Danes reached far more suicide verdicts than the English because they used criteria of probability rather than definite intent. The study showed that verdicts depend on coroners' decisions. Real suicide rates can never be known. Deaths may be accidental or, occasionally, murders. The view of suicide taken by a society, which often reflects the state religion, may influence the training of coroners and the verdicts that they believe will be acceptable. Interestingly, the researchers used a scientific approach, the controlled experiment, to show the weakness of another scientific approach — comparison of official statistics.

J. Douglas was another phenomenologist. In *The Social Meaning of Suicide* (1967), he argued that suicide should not be regarded as a single type of countable act because motives vary so much. It may be committed as an act of revenge, to say sorry or gain sympathy, to save the lives of others or to get swiftly to heaven (as in suicide cults). The best way to investigate this further would be to conduct interviews with survivors or with the families of suicide victims and to study diaries and suicide notes, all of which are interpretive methods.

In *Acta Psychiatrica* (1955), Ettlinger and Flordah studied the situations in which 500 cases of serious deliberate self-harm took place. Only 4% took precautions against discovery, indicating definite intent; 7% of cases were very unlikely to result in death, indicating that the people's intentions to kill themselves were not serious. Therefore, in 89% of cases, whether or not the individual would survive depended strongly on chance. This underlines the gamble involved in many attempted suicides, sometimes known as ludic suicides, and creates problems when definitions of suicide relate to definite suicidal intent. Like Atkinson and colleagues, these sociologists used figures to demonstrate the problems of basing theories on official statistics.

Case studies

In *The End of Hope* (1964), Kobler and Stotland carried out an interactionist case study of a mental hospital. They observed that an outbreak of suicides occurred when new suicide precautions were introduced. Patients interpreted this as evidence that staff saw their situation as hopeless, which apparently led to some patients taking their own lives.

While this was a primary study, some sociologists prefer to analyse secondary accounts of past cases. Baechler, in *Suicides* (1979), used existing case studies to classify suicides and attempted suicides into various types. Taylor conducted his own analysis of statistics of people killed under trains (1982) and showed that the figures were unreliable. Later, describing himself as a realist, he took a case study approach and identified four major causes of suicide. Details of the types of suicide identified by Baechler and Taylor are well summarised in Haralambos and Holborn's *Sociology: Themes and Perspectives* (2004). Analysing published case studies provides useful variety and avoids the ethical problems of interviewing survivors and distressed families. However, its value depends on the validity and completeness of the accounts used.

Conclusion

This brief survey of suicide studies should clarify the application of different theoretical approaches to a particular form of deviance. While studying suicide has its own specific problems, particularly the lack of witnesses and ethical sensitivity, parallels can be drawn with positivist, realist and phenomenological studies of other types of crime and deviance.

Task 8.2

As most of this chapter is a drawing together of threads, a summary has not been provided:

- Make a chart summarising the relative advantages of official, victim survey and self-report crime statistics.
- Produce a mind map of suicide studies, creating branches relating to the theoretical approaches described above. Add further examples from wider reading.

Task 8.3

Make notes for the following question, adapted from AQA.

Examine some of the problems of using qualitative methods and sources of data to study deviance. (12 marks)

Guidance

- Ensure that your essay begins with a definition and examples of qualitative methods, showing that you understand interpretivism and interactionism.
- This question implies a contrast with quantitative methods. Consider the limitations of:
  - observation
  - unstructured interviews
  - semiological interpretation of documents

Compare these with scientific methods, without discussing the latter at length. Besides the obvious lack of numerical data, refer to subjectivity, small samples and problems of comparison. Qualitative methods may impress the public less than a display of 'hard facts'.

- Remember that deviance includes suicide, crime, youth subcultures and mental illness. Discuss at least one named study in relation to each qualitative method. Use the PET mnemonic to consider other problems, searching Becker's list for further points.
- An appropriate summing up would emphasise theoretical problems and refer briefly to ethical and practical problems.

Useful websites

- S-cool! Revision site (follow leads to sociological topics you require)
  www.s-cool.co.uk/default.asp
- Home Office site describing British Crime Survey with links to statistics
  www.homeoffice.gov.uk/rds/bcs1.html
- Summaries of findings by the University of Oxford Centre for Suicide Research
  www.psychiatry.ox.ac.uk/csr/research.html

Further reading

- Haralambos, M. and Holborn, M. (2004) *Sociology: Themes and Perspectives*, HarperCollins.

- Lawson, T. and Heaton, T. (1999) *Crime and Deviance: Skills Based Sociology*, Macmillan.
- Swale, J. (2003) 'Suicide: a synoptic approach', in *Sociology Review*, Vol. 12, No. 4, pp. 26–28, Philip Allan Updates.
- Taylor, S. (1989) *Suicide*, Longman.

Final note

Although this book has focused primarily on deviance and crime, it is important to consider their less exciting opposites: conformity and law-abiding behaviour. While Marxists and social constructionists question the validity of conventional values and the criminal justice system, most ordinary citizens value conformity. Dull as it sounds, it enables them to plan their lives and go about their daily business without too many nasty surprises!

Glossary

accommodation
adaptation by immigrants to aspects of the host community's way of life, but without complete assimilation

administrative criminology
an approach that recommends practical measures to reduce crime

amplification of deviance
increase in actual or perceived deviance in reaction to a social response

anomie
lack of agreement over norms (Durkheim) or strain between approved goals and means (Merton)

antisocial behaviour order (ASBO)
statutory measure that aims to protect the public from behaviour that causes alarm or distress

argot
distinctive slang associated with particular subcultures

bonds
forms of attachment to society that discourage deviant behaviour

bourgeoisie
Marxist term for the ruling class and owners of the means of production

bricolage
creative and unconventional selection of items not usually found together; an expression of style

capitalism
an economic system dominated by privately owned businesses

chivalry thesis
the view that the police, magistrates and judges treat females leniently

cognitive maps
familiar routes, relating to the tendency to commit crime in the local area

commodity fetishism
capitalist condition in which material possessions are almost worshipped

communism
an economic system in which the state controls collective businesses and farms, so that those who work there share the profits of their labour

conformity
following social norms of behaviour

consensus/community policing
local police, often on foot, intending to become familiar and approachable figures

consensus theorists
sociologists who maintain that people need to be socialised to support agreed values and the law

control theory
the idea that people will commit crime unless they are either bonded to society or can be controlled formally

corporate crime
illegal acts of omission or commission by members of a legitimate organisation to increase its profits or influence

counterculture
a subculture opposing mainstream values

crime
behaviour that breaks the laws of a society

crimogenic
relating to factors that encourage crime

cultural heterogeneity
diversity of cultural background

cultural transmission
absorption of prevailing norms and values, such as deviant values in a particular locality

decode
interpret style or text using semiological methods

deviance
behaviour differing from the norms of a particular group or society

deviancy amplification spiral
continuing escalation of socially unacceptable behaviour in reaction to increasingly negative responses by media, police or other agents of control

deviant career
a fixed pattern of abnormal behaviour, often as a result of labelling

differential association
Sutherland's view that picking up deviant values from locality depends on a variety of factors

drift
Matza's theory that juvenile offences are usually unplanned

ecological theories
theories relating to the effects of the environment

environmental theories
theories relating crime rates to features of different localities

ethical
moral

ethnicity
identification with a specific culture, including religious practices and beliefs, languages spoken, dress, other customs and aspects of heritage

false consciousness
a Marxist term describing the way members of the proletariat are fooled into the acceptance of social inequalities by capitalist ideology

folk devils
people stigmatised in a moral panic

gated communities
residential areas with security measures designed to exclude strangers

gatekeeper
key member of a gang or group, who provides access and information for researcher

globalisation
the intensification of worldwide social relations — for example, rapid international communication

hegemony
social control that reinforces public support of capitalist values through manipulation of capitalist-controlled media and other institutions, for example schools

ideology
a set of beliefs, possibly false or biased

illegitimate opportunity structure
a local subculture supporting crime, gang culture or retreatist behaviour

innovation
Merton's word for crime

integration
being bonded into society

interactionist
a sociologist whose methods involve studying the way people interpret each other's actions and react accordingly

Islamophobia
irrational dislike or fear of Muslims

izzat
a concept of family honour, central to Islamic culture, that particularly influences the behaviour of women

labelling
public application of a negative description, such as 'offender', to a relatively powerless individual

Left realism
a socialist approach that acknowledges the need to reduce working-class crime

libertarians
conservatives who believe that laws should be limited to those intending to prevent people from harming others

ludic suicide
deliberately gambling with life and death by taking an extreme risk

macrosociology
a theory about whole societies, not necessarily based on empirical data

magic
an illusory feeling that subcultural style or symbolic violence expresses real power

malestream sociology
a study with a male bias

master status
a predominant personal identity — for example, as a serious deviant

microsociology
a small-scale empirical study

middle-range theory
a medium-scale study of groups within society that draws on empirical data but involves some generalisation

military-style/conflict policing
an approach making, typically, maximum use of cars, surveillance and heavy-handed stop-and-searches of stereotypically suspect groups

moral entrepreneurs
committed campaigners, usually aiming for a change in legislation

moral panic
public fear that is disproportionate to the actual threat; usually media-led

new criminology
a perspective combining Marxist structuralist analysis with smaller-scale interactionist focus

New Right
current conservative thinkers with a consensus perspective **norm** a useful form of behaviour is a particular context, accepted by society

norm
a useful form of behaviour in a particular context, accepted by society

normlessness
lack of agreement over values

objectivity
neutrality

oppositional values
priorities conflicting with those of mainstream society

orientalism
term used by Edward Said to refer to the supposedly commonly held view of Westerners that people from the East are inferior and 'other'

paternalists
those believing that the state should protect the vulnerable through laws that prevent them from harming themselves

pathological
   abnormal; the metaphor relates to sickness, implying that the offender risks contaminating others with antisocial behaviour

phenomenologists
   sociologists interested in people's constructions of phenomena such as crime

positivists
   sociologists who use 'scientific' methods'

primary deviation
   the first act of rule breaking

primary methods
   methods that involve the researcher generating new data

proletarianisation
   becoming more working class

proletariat
   Marxist term for the working class or wage labourers

rational choice theory
   the view that people weigh up the pros and cons of committing crime

realists
   sociologists interested in general trends, yet cautious of statistics, and also willing to use less clear-cut data

reintegrative shaming
   encouraging offenders to recognise and compensate for harm done, in exchange for being accepted back into the community

relative deprivation
   the experience of having less access to material goods than is the norm in one's society

reliability
   the likelihood that if study was replicated by another researcher in similar circumstances, similar results would be obtained

retreatism
   opting out of society

ritualism
   conforming closely to the rules of society for the satisfaction it brings

sanction

a punishment or reward

secondary deviation

serious departure from norms, resulting from being labelled for an earlier act

secondary methods

methods using the interpretation or comparison of pre-existing data

self-fulfilling prophecy

a prediction about a person's future that actually has the effect of creating the predicted outcome

semiology

a qualitative research method that 'reads' youth styles and media texts, usually for political meanings

situational crime prevention

discouragment of crime by practical local measures

social cohesion

integration of individuals within a society; feeling of unity

social construction

the varying way in which a phenomenon might be viewed by different groups

social disorganisation

lack of informal and formal social control, usually resulting in deviance

social regulation

control of individuals — for example, by surveillance and laws

state–corporate crimes

illegal arrangements made between a state and a TNC

state crime

an act by government agencies that breaks either the state's own criminal law or international law

strain theory

tension resulting from a mismatch between people's goals and socially approved means to reach them

style

outfit, music and patterns of behaviour associated with youth subculture

style tribe
a group of people adopting particular outfits for reasons of taste

subculture
a social, ethnic, economic or age group within a culture or society, but with a particular character of its own

subterranean values
baser instincts, usually repressed by most people

symbolic power
the illusion of being powerful — for example, gaining attention through shocking dress

symbolic violence
an act with the appearance of violence, usually to impress the peer group and appear powerful

target hardening
taking precautions at likely sites of crime — for example, using anti-theft devices

techniques of neutralisation
supplying reasons for why an act of deviance was justified

territoriality
subcultural attachment to a local area, often expressed through gang fights and confrontational support of a football team

time horizon
James Q. Wilson's idea about the length of time a person can wait before gratifying desires

tipping
loss of the good reputation of an area

transnational corporations (TNCs)
companies operating in several countries

triangulation
use of more than one research method

underclass
a group of largely unemployed people below the unskilled working class in status and prospects

validity
presentation of a true reflection of reality in a study

verstehen
empathising with the perspective of those studied

white-collar crime
offence(s) committed for personal profit by high-status people in the course of their occupations

world government
a government that could impose international law

yardies
gangsters from impoverished backyards of Kingston, Jamaica

youth culture
shared experience of most young people in a particular society

zero tolerance
discouragement by police and community wardens of public acts that are not necessarily illegal but that bring down the moral tone of an area

zone of transition
zone 2 of a city; a crime-prone area inhabited by the poor and by temporary residents